Principles of Negotiation

- Strategies
- Tactics
- Techniques to Reach Agreements

Editorial director: Jere L. Calmes
Cover design: Desktop Miracles, Inc.
Composition and production: MillerWorks

Advisory Editor for the Entrepreneur Press Legal Guide Series: Helen Cicino

Scales ©Rzymu

Library of Congress Cataloging-in-Publication Data

Guasco, Matthew P.
   Principles of negotiation : strategies, tactics, resolution (with CD-ROM)
/ by Matthew P. Guasco and Peter R. Robinson.
      p. cm. — (Entrepreneur legal guide series)
   Includes bibliographical references.
   ISBN 1-59918-138-X (alk. paper)
      1. Negotiation in business—Handbooks, manuals, etc. 2. Entrepreneurship.
      I. Robinson, Peter R. II. Title.
HD58.6.G83 2007
658.4'052—dc22   2007030410

Printed in Canada

12 11 10 09 08 07   10 9 8 7 6 5 4 3 2 1

Entrepreneur
MAGAZINE'S

LEGAL GUIDE

Matthew P. Guasco and Peter R. Robinson
Attorneys at Law

Principles of Negotiation

Entrepreneur
Press

- Strategies
- Tactics
- Techniques to Reach Agreements

Additional titles in Entrepreneur's *Legal Guides*

Helen Cicino, Esq.
Managing Editor

Bankruptcy for Businesses: The Benefits, Pitfalls and Alternatives

Business Contracts: Turn Any Business Contract to Your Advantage

Business Structures: How to Form a Corporation, LLC, Partnership, Sole Proprietorship (Available November 2007)

Estate Planning, Wills and Trusts

Forming an LLC: In Any State

Forming a Partnership: And Making It Work

Harassment and Discrimination: And Other Workplace Landmines (Available November 2007)

Hiring and Firing

Incorporate Your Business: In Any State (Available October 2007)

Intellectual Property: Patents, Trademarks, Copyrights, Trade Secrets (Available November 2007)

The Operations Manual for Corporations (Available November 2007)

The Small Business Legal Tool Kit

Small Claims Court Guidebook (Available January 2007)

Tax Planning for Business: Maximize Profit, Minimize Taxes (Available December 2007)

Contents

Preface

We all negotiate. Every day, in our lives and in our work, we negotiate. At times, we do it consciously, and other times we negotiate without knowing we are doing it at all. Negotiating is the lifeblood of all businesses. It is hard to imagine commerce without negotiation.

Yet, are you comfortable negotiating? Do you enjoy it? Do you fear it? Is it something you look forward to or something you dread? Are you aware of the way you negotiate, the tendencies you have which may make for good or bad deals? Do you negotiate instinctively, or do you negotiate strategically? Do you give much thought to negotiating at all?

The secret to effective negotiating has to do with answering these fundamental questions about yourself. All great negotiators know themselves and conduct their negotiations accordingly. Getting better deals begins with managing yourself and developing strategies that work. This book identifies the principles, strategies, and techniques of effective negotiating which the most successful negotiators have mastered. You can master them too.

Unlike other subjects in business and the law, negotiation does not have a clear set of rules to guide us. After all, negotiating is a process of communication between two or more people trying to reach agreement: The deal is the product of human interaction, understanding, personality, knowledge, power, language, and so many more variables. There is no single best way to negotiate. There are different styles of negotiating, each with its own benefits and disadvantages depending on the situation. If there is one secret to selecting the best negotiating strategy, it is this: It all depends on the unique circumstances of the people and the deal.

So how do you become a better negotiator? We have developed a method that looks at negotiation as the human communication process it is. You will learn about the following:

- the structure of the negotiation process
- competitive negotiating and its predictability
- how negotiators send and receive signals strategically in competitive negotiating
- the limitations of competitive negotiating and how to cooperatively negotiate for mutual gain
- the tactics negotiators employ and how to deal with them
- negotiator ethics and how to deal with challenging negotiating situations.

Most importantly, you will learn about the kind of negotiator you are and how you can manage yourself to success in any negotiation.

Our method draws from research in the fields of communication theory, psychology, game theory, sociology, linguistics, conflict resolution, and negotiation theory. We use specific examples to illustrate successful and ineffective negotiating techniques. You will find negotiating tips and review summaries to reinforce the information contained in each chapter and to assist you in your negotiations. We emphasize negotiating strategies and techniques that are of particular benefit to businesses large and small. Ultimately, however, it will be for you to learn through trial and error what works best for you. The deal is the ultimate measure of the effectiveness of the negotiator.

We hope this book helps you to become the best negotiator you can be. Better deals come from taking this journey of self-discovery.

Dedications

To Susan,
for her love, support, and understanding
during the writing of this book
and throughout our life together; and
to Emily and Anna,
the best daughters in the world.
—Matthew P. Guasco

To Vickie, Sara, Rachel, and Luke,
for your love, support, and patience
even when my obsession with negotiating
has been inconvenient or embarrassing.
—Peter R. Robinson

Acknowledgments

The authors wish to thank and acknowledge the many people who have preceded them in studying and describing the principles, strategies, and tactics of negotiation, and upon whose work they have relied in writing this book: L. Randolph Lowry, the founder of the Straus Institute for Dispute Resolution at Pepperdine University School of Law; Professor Charles B. Wiggins at the University of San Diego School of Law; and Bryan Johnston, former Associate Dean and Director of the Center for Dispute Resolution at Williamette University School of Law. The partnership of these influential scholars

over twenty years ago produced an innovative curriculum for teaching negotiation skills, which has played a formative role in the authors' conceptual-
ization of this book.

The work of these scholars and our own, of course, has drawn upon the
important contributions of others in the field of negotiation theory and practice,
including Roger Fisher, William Ury, David Lax, James Sebenius, Howard
Raiffa, Robert Axelrod, and Eleanor Holmes-Norton. Additionally, this book
was influenced considerably by the work of the following visiting and adjunct
faculty of the Straus Institute for Dispute Resolution at Pepperdine University
School of Law: Nina Meierding, Robert O'Donnell, Gerald Williams, Russell
Korobkin, Richard Coleman, and Bruce Myerson.

We would also like to express our gratitude and thanks to the administra-
tion, faculty, and staff of the Pepperdine University School of Law, whose support has been and continues to be the rock upon which our study and teaching
of the theory, principles, strategies, and techniques of negotiation are built.

Finally, we would like to express our profound thanks and undying gratitude
to Susan B. Lascher for her expert editing advice and assistance, which were
invaluable to the writing of this book. We would also like to thank Jere Calmes
and his staff at Entrepreneur Press, who had the idea which served as the spark
for what has turned out to be one of the more enjoyable experiences in our lives.

CHAPTER 1

Getting Started

What Every Negotiator Should Know
Before the Negotiation Begins

Before we examine how the entrepreneur or small business owner can negotiate better deals, we have to take a moment to look at the big picture. Effective negotiating begins with certain fundamental truths about what negotiation is and how we approach it, whether we are consumers buying a car, Fortune 500 executives considering a merger, or owners of a delicatessen dealing with a supplier. All deals, great and small, are influenced by how we think of and approach negotiating.

When we negotiate, do we give much thought to what we are doing? Too often, we think only about the end result—did we reach a deal or not? We spend little time thinking about *how* we got to that result or about the nature of the negotiating process itself. Yet, mastering the negotiation *process* has everything to do with getting better deals. Regrettably, we are often controlled *by* the negotiation process rather than being in control *of* it. The point of this book is to understand the negotiating process better so that you can manage it more effectively and improve the results of your negotiations—the deals you make. To do that, we must look at what happens with people when they negotiate.

Substance and Process:"How" is More Important than "What"

There are two aspects to every negotiation: the *substance* and the *process*. When negotiating a lease, for example, you need to determine the maximum amount of rent per square foot you are willing to pay. That is the "substance" of the negotiation, the tangible thing or the "what" that is being negotiated. Similarly, when you are buying an inventory of refrigerators, you must determine the amount you are willing to pay for them. Again, this is the *substance* of the negotiation. To negotiate a good deal, you must possess adequate knowledge of the substance of the negotiation. Knowledge of the value of the product, service, or property being exchanged is essential to reaching a good deal. It may take years of experience in a given business or profession to acquire such knowledge, or the prepared negotiator may learn sufficient information about the substance of the negotiation from study and research—checking with suppliers and other sellers, internet research, studying the classified ads in the newspaper. The *substance*—the what—of negotiating is always important.

> **Negotiating Tip**
>
> Every negotiator should know the substance of the negotiation = what the negotiation is about.

Many negotiators assume that expertise in the substance of the negotiation is all that is required to end up with better deals. For these negotiators, the negotiating *process*, that is, "how" the negotiation is conducted, is something they just do not think much about. Yet the substance of the negotiation only tells the negotiator of the possible ending points if agreement is reached—a good deal or a bad deal, fair market value or wholesale. The nature of negotiating, however, is that a deal will only be reached if the negotiators agree that the terms are desirable ending points for them both. If we do not understand the negotiation process, that is, how to negotiate strategically and effectively, we may not know how to get to the desired ending point or destination—the best deal possible.

> **Negotiating Tip**
>
> Every negotiation involves two components:
> Substance
> (what is being negotiated)
> and Process
> (how the parties negotiate).

With that in mind, the first and most fundamental step in getting better deals is to recognize that the process by which people negotiate (the how) is more important than the thing being negotiated (the what). The best negotiators are masters of the negotiation process. That is how they consistently get better deals, regardless of their knowledge of the subject matter of their negotiations. Successful negotiators, whether they own small businesses or large multinational corporations, are students of the negotiating process. They use their superior knowledge of the negotiating process to their advantage in getting good deals.

When Negotiations Go Bad

To demonstrate the importance of the negotiating process, consider this classic case study of a negotiation that went wrong. We have changed the names and facts to protect the identities of those involved.

Some years ago, a successful football player asked his agent to negotiate a renewal of his contract with a professional football team. The owner of the team (who we'll call Mr. Smith), a very successful and wealthy businessman in his own right, met with the agent.

As the negotiation began, the agent said, "Mr. Smith, my client would very much like to continue playing for the team. We feel he's an important part of its success. We also think he brings fans into the stadium."

He continued. "My client's present contract pays $175,000, but the market is very hot now, and we propose a one-year contract at $385,000." The agent smiled. "My client has earned the raise, and it will be a sound investment for your organization."

The owner was silent and looked right at the agent. After a moment, he said, "Young man, your client is getting old. His knees are shot, his rushing production is down, and I doubt he'll make it through the season." He paused, and then sighed. "But, then again, he's been a loyal player, and he's a good guy. Okay. Now, do you want to write it up, or shall I?"

The agent seemed pleased. "Well, Mr. Smith, we're making great progress. But you see, we want that one year contract *guaranteed*." The owner did not flinch, but stared impassively at the agent for an uncomfortably long time. He then said, "Young man, that's a lot to ask. You want me to pay him even if he's injured the first game?" The owner paused a bit longer. Finally, he sighed, and said, "Okay, young man. The year is guaranteed. *Now*, do you want to write it up, or shall I?"

The agent was elated. "Well, Mr. Smith, we're making great progress," he said. "But, we'd like to renew the contract for a second year at $525,000. The fans will appreciate the team's commitment to my client, and my client can finish his career here. It would be a really wise move on your part if we did that now." The owner frowned. He did not speak, but seemed to be pondering something. After a long silence, he said, "Very well, young man, first year guaranteed at $385,000, and renewal for a second year at $525,000. Now, do you want to write it up, or shall I?"

The agent smiled even more widely. "We're making great progress. But my client wants the second year guaranteed, just like the first." The owner said nothing.

The agent, sensing the mood had become icy, broke the silence. "I'm not sure you heard me," he said. The owner had in fact heard him, and he said only one word: "No." The agent's face wrinkled with concern. "Um... Mr. Smith, perhaps a guarantee on the second year was a *bit* much. The second year at $525,000 will be fine without the guarantee, and I'll write it up at that." The owner said only one word: "No."

The agent began sweating perceptibly. He hoped his malpractice insurance was up to date. "You're right, the second year can be worked out later. We'll just do the one year at $385,000, guaranteed, and we're done." The owner got up and said, "Young man, you're not understanding me. The answer is 'No.' Your client will never wear my team's uniform again. Now get out of my office."

For the last 15 years, the authors have asked thousands of students in our negotiation skills workshops to diagnose what went wrong with this negotiation. These students have provided many answers to this question, including the following:

- The agent got greedy.
- There was no give and take.
- The agent lacked judgment of when to accept a good deal for both parties.
- The agent should have put all the demands on the table at the beginning instead of surprising the owner with additional demands as the negotiation progressed.
- The agent insulted the owner.
- The player should have negotiated for himself or at least have been present.
- The owner took the negotiation personally.
- The owner should not have allowed his emotions to cloud his professional judgment and objectives.
- The owner encouraged the agent's insatiability by agreeing too easily to the early requests.
- The agent did not know his opponent.

None of our workshop participants responded, "I happen to have the expertise to determine the market value of this particular football player in the year of this negotiation, and, therefore, I can critique this negotiation based on the amount that this player actually should have been paid." That is the

Substance = What
(the desired outcome)

Process = How
(getting the other person to
agree to that outcome)

"What" of negotiation, the "substance." But also notice that even though the participants did not have the expertise to evaluate the professional services at issue, they still had many observations about why this negotiation was unsuccessful. Their observations were about the negotiation process—the how, not the what. The participants correctly identified that negotiations succeed or fail based on the *process*, not the *substance*, of the negotiation. That insight applies whether the negotiation is about your lease, the purchase of equipment, a salary package, or how many days you will spend with your in-laws this Christmas.

Effective negotiators are masters of process as well as substance. Making better deals involves skillful and strategic use of the negotiation process.

The Key to Getting a Good or Bad Deal: Manage or Be Managed

In the business world, people negotiate every day with little or no instruction about how to do it. It is simply assumed that they know how to negotiate or somehow they will figure it out as they go. Insurance adjusters are expected to negotiate with attorneys and injured parties concerning the payment of money for personal injuries and property losses. Sales professionals are taught the nature and benefits of the products they are asked to sell. As a small business owner, you know the specifics of the product or service you are selling, the details of financial management, and how to market your product or service. But you probably have received little or no guidance about how to negotiate the sale of your products or services. And yet, management of your business requires you to negotiate every day with clients, customers, and suppliers. You are a professional negotiator whether you know it or not. Like most professional negotiators, however, you gain experience and develop your negotiating style with little thought or training about *how* to negotiate. You do what works for you. If it's not broken, don't fix it, right?

Wrong. To negotiate better deals for your business, you must do more than simply negotiate by intuition or habit. You must be a student of the negotiation process. Entrepreneurs who are students of the negotiating process routinely get better deals. Organizational development experts have long agreed that businesses that study and understand management and communication processes can improve their performance in those processes. Organizational development and management consultants have helped make small and large businesses run more efficiently and profitably by educating those businesses about the management and communication processes. Knowledge first, mastery second.

The negotiation process, like management or marketing theory, does not have hard and fast rules to follow. Instead, there are different ways to negotiate, and there are many factors that are involved in the negotiating process. Some books insist there is a single way to negotiate. Some books seem to exhort you to "Be a Monster Negotiator," while others take a softer approach to negotiating, such as "The Peace and Beauty of Cooperative Negotiation." We believe that negotiating is a complex communication process between two people, which requires their mutual agreement to succeed. There is no one failsafe way to negotiate successfully. Instead, great negotiators have mastered many techniques to manage this complex communication process. Super negotiators do not negotiate the same way all the time. They strategically tailor their approaches to the unique negotiating situations they encounter. And the key to being able to do this is understanding how the negotiating process works. All negotiating wisdom comes from this simple premise.

The successful negotiator's two favorite words are "adaptability" and "flexibility." How you negotiate the sale of your product to a good customer may be different from how you negotiate with a customer with whom you have never done business. How you negotiate the purchase of supplies from a vendor may be different from how you negotiate with your business partner concerning a buy-out of his interest. How you negotiate with your child about who should get the last cookie hopefully will differ from the negotiation you have with your landlord concerning renewal of your lease. Good negotiators are flexible and adaptable: They shape the negotiating process to the situation. Because of that, there are no rigid rules governing how you negotiate. Rather than suggesting that there are, this book creates a conceptual roadmap to help you identify the types of strategic decisions, choices, and dilemmas faced by the conscious negotiator, the negotiator who is aware of and understands the dynamics of the negotiating process. Our goal is to help you transform your approach to negotiating from an unconscious, reactive behavior to a consciously managed strategy.

Negotiating Tip

The best negotiators are students of the negotiation process and they are adaptable and flexible.

It may help to think of the negotiation process as being similar to taking a trip by car from one city to another. The person who manages the process is the driver of the car. The driver assumes the responsibility of making countless strategic decisions required to drive the car to the desired destination: accelerating, slowing, turning, braking, avoiding other cars and trucks, exiting the freeway, entering the freeway, merging, and abiding by a host of traffic laws. We like to think of successful negotiators as good drivers; they manage the countless strategic choices and decisions in the negotiation process to achieve the desired outcome, getting to the destination safely, if you will. Alternatively, many negotiators simply choose to be passengers; they do not drive the process, but are driven during it. It is easier and requires much less effort to be the passenger in the negotiation process: Passengers do not have to pay attention to nearly as many details or make as many decisions as do drivers. But such passivity often comes at the price of a less desirable outcome. To continue the metaphor, the passenger has no control over the destination or whether he will arrive there safely. The passenger is at the mercy of the driver.

In the football contract negotiation discussed earlier, who was the driver and who was the passenger? Was the agent the driver? The agent's client did not return to the team he loved. It turns out that few teams were interested in the client, who ended up playing four games for another team before being forced to retire due to injury. He earned only $85,000 as opposed to the $525,000 to which the owner had agreed. His agent might have been comfortable with the way he negotiated in this instance, but the client was not happy and a deal did not occur. The agent was either clueless about or seriously misjudged the negotiation process. If he was the driver, the car went over a cliff.

What about the owner? Was he equally uninformed about the negotiation process? Many sports writers at the time thought otherwise. People who knew this owner believed that he was looking for a way to kill the deal because the star player was well past his prime. It did not make business sense to pay the player what he wanted, but the fans would have been insulted if the owner had not at least tried to renew the contract of a loyal and beloved player. So the owner found a way to get out of the deal by giving the agent all the rope he needed to hang himself: The owner agreed too easily to the first two demands, which led the agent to greedily ask for one too many concessions. And the owner was able to truthfully tell the community, "I did everything I could. I even offered to increase the player's salary, guarantee him the first year, and increase it the second year. But I had to draw the line there. Because if I don't, then what would other healthier players want, and how much would I have to increase ticket prices to pay their extravagant demands? After all, I have to look out for the interests of you, our loyal fans."

Looking at the negotiation this way, the owner was the driver, and the agent was the passenger. In fact, the owner was a really good driver. The agent was outmaneuvered. The owner was not crazy after all. He was crazy like a fox. The owner manipulated the negotiation process to induce the agent into asking for too much so that the owner could credibly tell the team's fans that the player had turned down a generous compensation package. Not reaching a deal with this player had superior value for the owner, who saved his money and spent it on younger, healthier players who could help the team more than this older player would have been able to do. The agent blew a guaranteed one-year renewal at a substantial pay raise, as well as a second year with even more money. The owner successfully drove the car to his intended destination. On the way, he politely shoved the agent, and by implication the player, out the door and over a cliff.

> **Negotiating Tip**
>
> Negotiating success means knowing yourself. Are you a driver or a passenger?

Frequently, the negotiation process manages us more than we manage it. We say and do things during a negotiation that we have a hard time understanding later. How did that happen? How did I get there? Sometimes one negotiator manages the process to the detriment of the other. A simple negotiating equation may help one to manage, rather than be managed by, the negotiation:

> Strategy + Self-Management + Information = Negotiation Power = **Driver**
>
> No Strategy + Reaction + Lack of Information = Negotiation Weakness = **Passenger**

Thus, the first step in getting better deals is to develop a negotiating strategy, a game plan or roadmap if you will. Effectively following a roadmap, in turn, depends on your ability to think strategically while the negotiation is happening, managing yourself and the other negotiator in the process. Manage or be managed, that is the mantra of every successful negotiator. Good negotiators are good drivers, not passengers, during the negotiation process.

The next time you are buying equipment or supplies for your business, or negotiating with a customer for one of your products, or marketing your services to a potential client, ask yourself this question: Am I being the driver in this negotiation, or the passenger? This insight alone will help you begin the process of managing, as opposed to being managed by, the negotiation.

Decision Making in the Face of Uncertainty

There is one problem with equating mastery of the negotiation process to good driving with a strategic roadmap. No matter how well prepared we are, negotiating always involves decision making in the face of uncertainty. It is impossible to know everything your negotiating partner thinks or might do. Preparation can reduce, perhaps substantially, the uncertainty in a negotiation, but there is always something the negotiator does not know. If you walk away from a deal with the vendor of ink-jet cartridges for your business's printers, will the vendor come back to you with a better price? Or will the vendor be able to sell the same or greater volume of ink-jet cartridges to another purchaser at the same or a higher price? What is the vendor's actual per-unit cost for the cartridges? Has the vendor had a good sales month or not? So, negotiating is like driving with a map that only has possible destinations on it:

Drivers of the negotiating process make their own roads to their most favored destinations, while passengers permit themselves to be driven to their least desirable destinations on the map.

The uncertainty inherent in each negotiation, while maddening, is also very revealing. It can show you what kind of negotiator you are, that is, whether you are most comfortable being the driver or the passenger. When we do not know what the other negotiator will do, that uncertainty forces us to guess and to make decisions based on those guesses. Using the above example, suppose the negotiation happens like this: The vendor contacts you and offers to sell you ink-jet cartridges that are compatible with your several printers for a per unit price of $27. At that moment, you can decide to do any of the following: 1) pay the price, 2) offer a lower price, or 3) say you are not interested. If you are interested in buying ink-jet cartridges for your business's printers, you have two choices: 1) pay the price, or 2) offer a lower price. If you offer a lower price, and the vendor proposes a counter-offer, you will have to decide how far to negotiate. When the vendor says "No," you will have to choose whether to walk away or pay the price. All the while, you will not know the lowest price the vendor will accept without negotiating with her. She will not know the highest price you will pay without negotiating with you. You both will be guessing what each of you will do as you negotiate with each other. All negotiations involve decision-making in this environment of uncertainty.

> **Negotiating Tip**
>
> Drivers manage the negotiating process to get better deals. Passengers let the negotiating process manage them, and they frequently get taken for a ride.

The inherent uncertainty of the negotiating process is most noticeable when you are unpleasantly surprised. For example, what if you respond to the vendor's offer by saying you will not pay more than $24.00 per cartridge, and the vendor counters with a price of $26.75? A common reaction many business owners have is to grow tired of the negotiating process, and offer to split the difference with the vendor. "Let's cut to the chase; I'll split the difference with you and pay $25.37 per cartridge, and I'll buy 25 cartridges." The vendor might agree, and the cartridges are yours. But, if the vendor responds by trying to negotiate between your reasonable offer and the vendor's last price, you might become irritated. Many people have this experience when negotiating; they describe the phenomenon as being "nickel and dimed." In this hypothetical situation, you would have misjudged the vendor's response—she did something you did not expect and that upset you. Yet, great negotiators successfully confront the uncertainty about what the other negotiator will do by forecasting the other negotiator's probable behaviors, very much the way chess is played. The strategic negotiator thinks, "If I do X, what do I think the other person will do?" The more accurate your forecasts, the more effective negotiator you will be. To get back to our driving analogy, all good drivers anticipate what other cars on the road might do and adjust accordingly.

> **Negotiating Tip**
>
> Negotiating is like playing chess. Plan your moves in advance and anticipate what you will do in response to the other negotiator's moves.

Forecasting the other negotiator's probable responses depends on what you learn about her before and during the negotiation. Still, no matter how well you know the other negotiator, you will always experience some level of uncertainty about what she will do during the negotiation. The factors affecting the level of such uncertainty are endless. How will the other person's responses be affected if I

- dress in a certain way?
- share or refuse to share certain information?
- hire a lawyer to negotiate this matter?
- host the meeting and serve generous refreshments?
- make a specific concession?
- make the first concession?
- walk away?
- get angry?
- get emotional?
- threaten to negotiate with someone else?

Both negotiators make decisions in this environment of uncertainty. How well they do in a negotiation depends upon how comfortable they are with the process of negotiating. It also depends on whether the negotiators are using the negotiating process as a way of gathering information about what each other will do. Strategic negotiators look for information in what the other negotiator says and does before and during the negotiation. The negotiation process requires both participants to guess what the other will do based upon this information. Your success as a negotiator hinges on your ability to accurately anticipate and interpret the behaviors of the other negotiator based upon his words and actions. In order to be the driver of the negotiation, you must create roads to destinations to which the passenger is willing to be driven. In order to do that, you must carefully anticipate and observe the other negotiator's actions. That information reduces your uncertainty, which increases your power to drive the negotiation in the direction you wish.

Managing the Mixed Motives of Competition and Cooperation

The uncertainty of what the other negotiator will do can help us understand whether we are innately competitive or cooperative.

In every negotiation, whether it involves the purchase of ink-jet cartridges or a contract for professional services, the negotiators have to balance two separate and conflicting motivations: whether to compete with each other for a scarce resource or whether to cooperate with each other to expand the available resources to meet each other's needs. Negotiation theorists call this the "Mixed Motive Exchange." We discuss the techniques of competitive negotiating in Chapter 2 and those of cooperative negotiating in Chapter 3. At this point, however, we want you to determine a fundamental truth about yourself that will influence your negotiations before they even begin: Are you naturally cooperative or competitive? Are you comfortable with competitive negotiating or do you view it as an evil to be avoided? Are you more comfortable negotiating cooperatively, or does your competitive nature make it hard for you to be

> **Negotiating Tip**
>
> The uncertainty of what the other negotiator will do can help us understand whether we are innately competitive or cooperative.

cooperative? These fundamental truths about yourself have everything to do with whether you routinely get good or bad deals in your negotiations.

People who are innately cooperative and dislike negotiating often blame their bad experiences on the people with whom they have negotiated. These people rarely blame the experience or the outcome of negotiating on themselves. We think they are in denial. Every negotiation requires you to make decisions without knowing what the other negotiator will do, and the one thing you can control is yourself. If you acknowledge that you cannot control the other negotiator's behavior, the next step in constructing your conceptual roadmap for negotiating is to understand the tension within you that you can control—your own mixed motives of competition and cooperation. Thus, it is very likely that these negotiating failures were not due to the behavior of the other negotiators at all. As Shakespeare wrote, "The fault lies not in our stars, but in ourselves."

> **Negotiating Tip**
>
> Good negotiators exercise control over the one thing in their power—themselves—and they learn to manage their own competitive and cooperative instincts.

To better understand how each negotiator must confront and manage his or her own mixed motives of cooperation and competition in a negotiation, consider the following scenario. Assume you need to sell your car. It is a nice car, in good condition, convertible, and it is cherry red. Your research suggests the car is worth $5,000, so you are willing to sell it for anything over that price. Therefore, you decide to advertise the car for $6,000 to leave yourself some negotiating room. You park the car on a very public street, and after placing the "For Sale" sign on it, you are about to write in the price. Before you can write "$6,000" on the sign, a car screeches to a halt nearby, the driver leaps out, and he runs up to you saying, "I had a car just like this when I was in high school. I have been trying to find one like it for over a year." He lovingly caresses the shiny red body with a faraway look in his eyes. He asks, "What do you want for it?"

As you contemplate your response, we hope you are having an internal debate. Without suggesting that you are losing your marbles, we hope you hear two voices at this moment. One of the voices is encouraging you to consider naming a price greater than $6,000. Your original idea was to advertise the car for $6,000, hoping to sell it for more than $5,000, but that was done in a vacuum. Now you have additional information that suggests you have a very motivated buyer who might be willing to pay a premium. Maybe if you started at $7,000, you could actually sell it for $6,000. Maybe if you started at $8,000, you could sell it for more than $6,000! The voice that advocates for pumping up your opening number represents the internal motive of competition.

The competitive motive in negotiation seeks to claim as much value as possible. This is what negotiation professionals refer to as a competition for a fixed pie. The pie is whatever the substance of the negotiation is: money, property, services. When there is a fixed pie of value, both negotiators must engage in some form of competition with each other in order to gain the biggest slice of the pie. One negotiator's gain will result in a corresponding loss for the other negotiator. In the car sale scenario, your competitive voice should be urging you to claim as much value—the biggest slice of the pie—as possible. You have an eager potential buyer. You might get more money than you thought was possible. The competitive motivation exploits that opportunity for gain.

There is nothing wrong or immoral about this motivation. In fact, an effective strategic negotiator should listen to his or her competitive voice. Competition is one of the motives the strategic negotiator must understand and manage. Often, the difference between keeping and losing one's job as a salesperson involves one's willingness or unwillingness to honor the competitive motivation. If your response to the potential car buyer's question is to ask for $6,000 or $5,000, you are innately cooperative. It is also likely that you do not like negotiating, and that you routinely receive less in your negotiations than might otherwise be the case if you negotiated competitively. You have rationalized being a passenger. You, more than anyone else reading this book, need to learn to become a driver!

The urge to compete, however, must be balanced with the contrasting motivation to be cooperative. Cooperation is inherent in the negotiation process because the other negotiator's consent is required to reach an agreement. The negotiation begins and continues as a result of the negotiators' voluntary participation in it. By its nature, negotiating requires sharing information and

Definition

Competitive negotiating is claiming the biggest slice of a fixed pie of value

perspectives, which involves cooperation to some extent. Effective cooperation in negotiation creates value, making the pie bigger so that both negotiators can meet their needs. Competitive negotiating assumes a fixed pie as to which one negotiator claims value in direct proportion to the other negotiator's loss of value. Cooperation is mutual gain for the negotiators. Competition is mutually exclusive gain by one negotiator at the expense of a concession made by the other negotiator. Good negotiators balance the mixed motives of cooperation and competition beautifully to achieve better deals. If you are too competitive, you can kill a deal because the other negotiator does not want to do business with you. If you are too cooperative, the other negotiator may take advantage of you.

In the scenario regarding the red car, the effective strategic negotiator should listen to his or her cooperative voice in addition to the competitive voice. If you are the seller, you do not want to alienate a potential buyer by being too competitive and setting the price at $15,000 for a car you are willing to sell for $5,000. If the price is unreasonably high, you might insult the potential buyer and cause him to get discouraged and leave. If you want to sell the car quickly for a reasonable price, allowing you to spend the weekend at the lake with your family, being strategically cooperative dictates setting a price that will make it easier to have a successful negotiation, such as $7,000 or $8,000. Thus, good negotiators effectively balance their competitive and cooperative motives in every negotiation. In particular, these negotiators know whether they are innately cooperative or competitive, and they manage themselves accordingly to maximize the value they receive in their negotiations. The negotiator's ability to strategically manage his or her own competitive or cooperative nature is the key to being the driver, not the passenger in any negotiation.

Negotiating Tip

Good negotiators temper competition with cooperation. Driving the car requires both assertiveness and prudence to get to your destination safely.

Managing the mixed motives of competition and cooperation is easier to say than to do. Most negotiators resolve the tension between the two unconsciously. Most people negotiate in conformity with their personalities. If a negotiator has a competitive personality, he or she is likely to negotiate competitively. If he or she is naturally cooperative, the negotiator will respond cooperatively. People tend to negotiate intuitively in a way that is most comfortable for them. Personality and intuition guide negotiating behavior, but not always to the best destinations.

To demonstrate how powerfully our naturally competitive or cooperative natures unconsciously influence our negotiating behaviors, try the following exercise. Cross your arms. Just do it the way that comes most naturally without thinking about it. Finished? Okay, now, put the top arm on the bottom and the bottom arm on the top—that is, fold your arms the opposite of the way you usually do it. When the students in our negotiating skills courses do this exercise, most of them find it difficult if not impossible to fold their arms any differently than the way they normally do it. This demonstrates the power of our comfort zones: We negotiate in ways that are natural and comfortable for us. Thus, we say and do things in negotiating without giving them much thought. It takes an effort of will to fold your arms in a different way than you have ever done it before. Similarly, it can be difficult to negotiate strategically, to learn to manage yourself in a way different than you have in prior negotiations.

> **Negotiating Tip**
>
> There is a simple phrase every negotiator should remember before each negotiation: Know thyself, then manage thyself to achieve success.

Whether you are innately cooperative or competitive, you can be an effective negotiator. Some competitive negotiators are regarded by their peers as being very successful. Similarly, some negotiators with cooperative styles are exceptionally effective. This should be comforting for anyone trying to evaluate his or her own negotiating personality: you do not need to change who you are in order to be an effective negotiator. You just have to learn who that person is and manage yourself accordingly. If you are naturally competitive, you need to learn how to be strategically cooperative. If you are naturally cooperative, you need to learn how to be strategically competitive.

It is important to note that you can be an effective negotiator if you have an intuitively competitive or cooperative approach. Both approaches have their strengths and weaknesses. Competitive negotiators tend to get really

FIGURE 1-1. **The Mixed Motive Exchange**

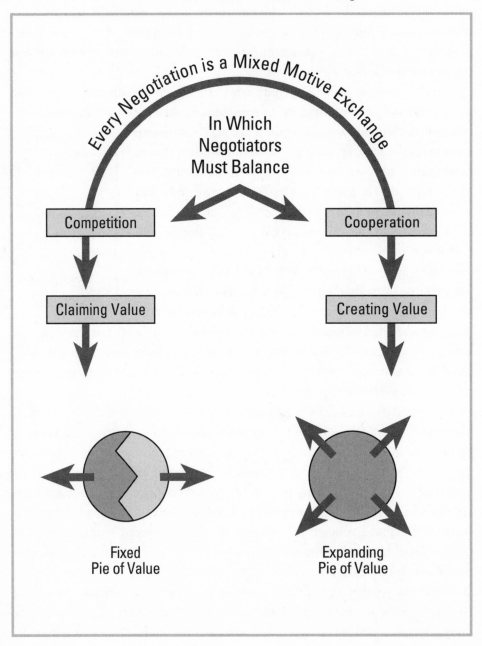

good deals. Unfortunately, if they are too competitive, they may fail to close many deals, and those who do business with them may not want to repeat the experience. Cooperative negotiators tend to reach deals more readily than competitive negotiators. Unfortunately, they may settle for less advantageous terms than would competitive negotiators. Being the nice guy may come at too great a price: a bad deal.

It is amazing how many negotiators simply come to the negotiation without a road map, without knowing their naturally competitive or cooperative tendencies, and react on the fly. Maybe things have worked out okay for them in the past, but the odds are very good that, if they are naturally cooperative, they have been taken before; and if they are naturally competitive, they have killed some deals. Success is getting what you need out of the deal.

Avoiding Exploitation: How a Cooperative Negotiator Can Manage a Competitive Negotiator

Much of the discussion in this chapter has focused on general concepts applicable to all negotiations. Strategic self-management of one's own cooperative or competitive nature is something all negotiators must do to be successful. A particular concern, however, arises for small business owners: How do I avoid being taken by a more competitive, adept negotiator? Fortunately, there is an approach all negotiators, including small business owners, can use to avoid being exploited.

The skilled negotiator must consider whether she makes appropriate decisions about when and how much to compete and cooperate. This strategic decision, in turn, depends upon how well you manage the behavior of the other negotiator. Remember, it is your job to be the driver, not the passenger. The other negotiator may (in fact should!) want to be the driver and have you be the passenger. Therefore, you must develop a strategy for remaining in control and encouraging the other negotiator to do what you need him or her to do in order to reach a deal.

Nobel Prize caliber mathematicians who specialize in something called "Game Theory" have studied the problem of how best to manage the mixed motives of competition and cooperation in a negotiation. The Academy Award-winning film *A Beautiful Mind* told the story of one such game theorist,

John Nash. Among other things, game theorists use complex mathematical equations and computer modeling to explore the variety of outcomes that occur as a result of the differing combinations of competition and cooperation in a negotiation. Their findings provide useful insights to us about how much competition and cooperation we might employ in a given negotiation. More importantly, the game theorists have come up with a model that helps us to manage our own competitive and cooperative tendencies, while at the same time managing those of the other negotiator. This is particularly good news for small business owners who negotiate with large suppliers or customers.

Robert Axelrod was a game theorist who focused on the process by which one could achieve a satisfactory result in a negotiation while avoiding the risk of exploitation inherent in being cooperative. The result of his efforts is a wonderfully simple, four-step rule for avoiding exploitation when balancing the motives of cooperation and competition in a negotiation. Unlike the work of many game theorists, which is incomprehensible to most of us, Axelrod's theory is easy to follow in any negotiation.

Step One: Begin Cooperatively

Axelrod's first suggestion is to begin a negotiation cooperatively. This is especially challenging for naturally competitive negotiators. A competitive beginning to a negotiation has a large probability of eliciting a competitive response. When this occurs, the die has been cast for that negotiation; both parties will negotiate competitively. Future interactions will remain competitive. Perhaps this is unavoidable in some negotiations, but the negotiator has a strategic choice here. An unnecessarily competitive and aggressive beginning to the negotiation will not only produce a similar response, but such negotiations quite frequently result in hostility and no agreement. Axelrod's suggestion to begin cooperatively recognizes that the negotiator who begins the negotiation has the power to influence the behavior of the other negotiator. Then the other negotiator has the option of responding cooperatively or competitively. That door would be closed with too competitive an initial move.

So how does a negotiator make a cooperative first move that does not risk being exploited by a more competitive negotiator? You might try beginning the negotiation by giving up something you can afford to lose. For example, you might give the other negotiator information you know he or she will eventually acquire, or you can offer a small concession that has little value to you. By making these gestures you give the other negotiator the opportunity to respond in kind, which will likely produce a fruitful negotiation. Do not begin *too* cooperatively. Trying the first step of Axelrod's theory does not mean revealing your bottom line or disclosing sensitive information in the hope the other negotiator will do likewise. A competitive negotiator would greet such a cooperative move as an invitation to exploit you.

For example, suppose you own a small appliance store. A new dishwasher has just arrived in your stock, and it is very attractive, stainless steel model with European design touches that are popular now. Before you have a chance to put a price tag on the floor model, a customer comes into your store and asks, "How much is this dishwasher?" You might respond by saying, "Well, it's a new model, and the list price is $1,250." This strikes the right balance between cooperation and competition: Your response invites a negotiation by stating that the dishwasher is "listed" at $1,250, thus leaving the door open to a lower price depending on the customer's offer... just enough cooperation in what is likely to be a competitive negotiation.

Step Two: If the Response is Competitive, Match the Move

Axelrod's second suggestion is that if your cooperative opening move in the negotiation meets with a competitive response, you must respond competitively. If you respond to a competitive negotiating move with a cooperative one, this is exactly the recipe for being exploited. The competitive negotiator will continue competing while you continue cooperating. The competitive negotiator will get all he or she wants and then some. You will come away from the negotiation with less than you need. The naturally cooperative negotiator must recognize when this is happening and consciously intervene to prevent it.

A word of caution to those of you who are naturally competitive and are tempted to unleash the mother of all competitive responses. Your reaction to a competitive move after you have opened cooperatively should be thoughtful, measured, and in proportion with that move. Too much of a competitive response and you can lock the negotiation in a fatally competitive dance. Too small of a competitive response and the other negotiator will not notice it. The purpose of matching the move is to discourage the other negotiator's competitive behavior and encourage him or her to adopt a more cooperative approach. That goal is not achieved by encouraging an escalation of competition. Matching the move means a measured reciprocal response that keeps the negotiation going but sends the signal that you are not going to be exploited.

For example, using the dishwasher negotiation example above, suppose the customer's response to your statement about the list price is something like, "I thought this was a discount appliance store. I would not pay more than $600 for that machine." You might be tempted to overreact and say, "Well, if you need that steep of a discount, may I recommend the thrift store down the street?" But that would not be matching the customer's competitive move with a proportionate competitive response. Instead, you might consider saying something like, "The list price is suggested by the manufacturer, and while I might consider a slightly lower price, $600 is out of the question." Matching the move means letting the other negotiator know that you can be competitive, too, but it also leaves the door open to a cooperative response from the other negotiator. Good negotiators open doors, they do not close them.

Step Three: If the Response is Cooperative, Match the Move

If you begin cooperatively and the other negotiator responds cooperatively, Axelrod suggests that you continue to make cooperative moves in the negotiation. Again, match the move. Mutual cooperation produces good results and neither negotiator is being exploited. Both negotiators are interested in sharing the proverbial pie, and they might even find ways of expanding the pie, creating value, and efficiently reaching durable and mutually satisfying agreements. This type of cooperative negotiating is referred to as Integrative Bargaining and will be discussed in greater depth in Chapter 3.

For example, in the dishwasher example above, suppose that, after you responded to the customer's $600 offer in the somewhat competitive manner suggested, the customer said, "Well, I suppose $600 is too good to be true. Would you take $800 for it?" The customer has sent you a cooperative signal.

It is time to reward this behavior by being cooperative. You might say, "We pride ourselves on the best prices for the best quality appliances. We can't sell a machine this excellent for $800, but I can sell it to you for $1,050." This is a cooperative signal along with a substantial price concession. The message is clear: "I like your last move and I want to reward it."

Some negotiators do not forgive so easily, however, and this is their Achilles heel: They might be tempted to respond to a cooperative signal with a competitive signal because they are still angry about the earlier competitive move. Thus, if you responded angrily to the $600 offer from the customer and you were not listening for her cooperative invitation to a negotiation for a higher price, you might say, "Obviously, you were not listening to me. I said the price is $1,250." Matching the move means encouraging cooperation and discouraging competition from the other negotiator. Negotiating is all about making deals, not killing them. Your task is to reward the other negotiator for doing what you want her to do and discouraging her from doing what you do not want her to do.

> **Negotiating Tip**
>
> Successful negotiators balance their own mixed motives of competition and cooperation, while at the same time discouraging the other negotiator from being too competitive.

Step Four: At All Stages, Be Clear and Consistent, But Flexible

The success of Axelrod's theory depends upon the negotiator making strategic choices from the beginning and throughout the negotiation. Most negotiations involve several moves before agreement is reached. At each step, the strategic negotiator avoids exploitation and impasse by sending clear and consistent signals. For example, the negotiator who begins cooperatively, then matches a competitive response with a competitive move, might signal a willingness to be exploited by making the next move too cooperative. Or, a naturally competitive negotiator might follow a cooperative move with too competitive a move and kill the deal. Clarity and consistency are the key to managing the other negotiator's expectations in order to reach agreement.

If there is one word that sums up Axelrod's theory of avoiding exploitation it is "flexibility." Strategic negotiators adapt and shape their moves to the developing conversation in the negotiation. In this way, effective negotiators manage the mixed motives of competition and cooperation to achieve agreements that meet their needs. While much of game theory involves complex mathematics, Axelrod's theory is simplicity itself: Design your negotiation moves in a way that sends signals encouraging the other negotiator to do what you want him to do and discouraging him from doing things you do not want him to do. Manage or be managed.

If you learn nothing else from this book, the key points below will help you negotiate better deals. Being an effective strategic negotiator, however, requires an in-depth understanding of both competitive and cooperative negotiating styles and techniques. For that, you will have to read on.

Key Points to Remember: Chapter 1

1. Negotiation is a process of communication involving two or more people attempting to reach agreement.

2. The process of the negotiation (how) is more important than the substance (what) in successful negotiations.

3. All negotiations involve decision-making in the face of uncertainty.

4. Every negotiator must manage the mixed motives of competition and cooperation.

5. The successful negotiator's mantra: know thyself and manage thyself accordingly.

6. The prime directive: manage or be managed.

7. Competitive negotiators keep dancing as long as the music is playing.

8. Cooperative negotiators resist dancing even though the night is still young.

9. Manage yourself and avoid exploitation by following Axelrod's theory of responding to the other negotiator's moves and sending clear and consistent signals in your moves.

10. You have the choice of being a driver rather than a passenger.

CHAPTER 2

Competitive Negotiating

Claiming Value in the Dance

In Chapter 1, we established that the strategic negotiator tries to manage herself and the other negotiator by balancing the competitive and cooperative natures of negotiation. The driver and the passenger is the perfect metaphor because that is what strategic negotiating is all about; good negotiators are masterful drivers with a specific destination and a map to get them there. In order to do that effectively, and to negotiate better deals, the strategic negotiator must understand the techniques of competitive negotiating. Chapter 3 focuses on cooperative bargaining, but this chapter is devoted solely to the nature and techniques of competitive negotiating.

Dividing a Fixed Pie

The defining characteristic of competitive negotiating is that the negotiators are trying to divide a fixed pie—the resource or value that is the subject of the negotiation—and each is trying to claim as much of the pie as possible. Many commentators refer to this approach to negotiation as "distributive bargaining" as the negotiators are trying to agree on a formula for distributing a fixed pie of resources between them. The fixed pie the negotiators are competing to divide can be any tangible thing, including money (e.g., the monthly payment on a lease), time (e.g., the duration of a lease), space (e.g., the number of square feet being leased), quantity (e.g., the number of entrances, offices, or electrical outlets in the space being leased), services (e.g., lawn care), and the list goes on. If you think about it, we encounter fixed-pie negotiations every day.

Where there is a fixed pie of value, and each negotiator is trying to claim as much of that pie as possible, the two negotiators engage in competitive negotiating to distribute that pie. There is nothing cooperative about competitive negotiating; if both negotiators were in a position to distribute the pie cooperatively, they would simply slice it in half and that would be the end of it. But the real world is not like that. If you are in the business of selling

FIGURE 2-1. **Competitive Negotiation**

Competitive Negotiation = Trying to Divide a Fixed Pie

Both negotiators claim as much value as possible,
trying to get the biggest slice of the pie.

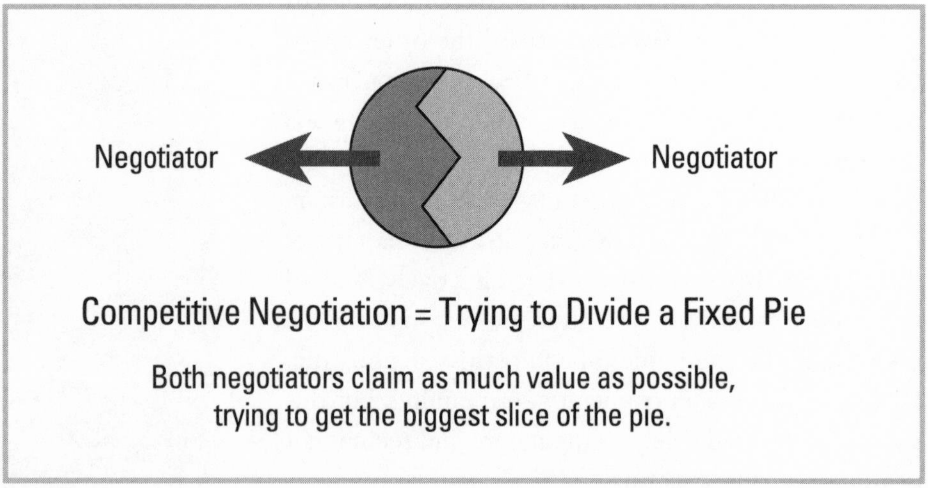

cars, will you be as profitable as possible by cooperating with buyers to split the difference with them in every negotiation? No. Instead, the success of your business depends on minimizing what you give and maximizing what you gain in your negotiations, which includes the purchase of inventory and equipment, or the sale of goods and services. To minimize the cost of doing business and to maximize profits, you must competitively negotiate to claim as much value as you can. Successful negotiators consistently get better deals by understanding and using competitive negotiating techniques strategically and effectively.

Understanding the Predictability of Competitive Negotiating

A key feature of competitive negotiating is its predictability. Effective negotiators maximize value in competitive negotiating by using that predictability to their strategic advantage.

Predicting anything is a powerful skill. When we can anticipate what will or may happen, uncertainty is reduced and we are more confident of our actions. Techniques that might have influenced a negotiator to accept a less advantageous deal are not as effective once she understands and anticipates those techniques.

Understanding the predictability of distributive/competitive bargaining is similar to watching a suspenseful movie the second time. The first time you view the movie, the tense scene or the surprise ending creates stress and tension; you may even scream or squirm in your seat at the climactic moment. The second time you see the film, however, you know what is coming, so you are more relaxed. When the tense moment comes, you are less affected by it because you know what will happen. Predictable things occur in a competitive negotiation. If you have studied the process, you know what is coming, and you will be more relaxed and less affected as it occurs. Better yet, you can use the predictability of competitive negotiating to encourage the other negotiator to act in a way that helps you get a better deal.

One benefit of understanding the predictability of competitive negotiating is the power that knowledge gives you to manage the other negotiator's expectations. As we discussed in Chapter 1, both negotiators must consent to the terms of the deal if the negotiation is to conclude with an agreement. The other negotiator will come to the negotiation with an idea of the range of acceptable terms for the deal. You get better deals by attempting to influence those expectations so that the other negotiator will accept less for himself and agree to more for you. Thus, a seller wants to manage the buyer's expectation so that the buyer will agree to a price higher than the one she thought she might pay, and a buyer wants to manage the seller's expectation so that the seller will accept a price lower than the one he thought he might get. If the buyer and seller are effective strategic negotiators, they will attempt to manage each other's expectations in order to get the best terms possible; that is, to claim the biggest slice of the pie.

Purchasing a Car:
The Predictability of Competitive Negotiating on Display

The best and simplest example of the strategic negotiator's use of the predictability of competitive negotiating to manage the other negotiator's expectations is one that occurs every day: the negotiation involved in the purchase of an automobile. We will describe a generic car buying negotiation to provide a picture of the predictability of competitive negotiating. While car buying experiences vary from region to region, nearly all such negotiations share the common feature of predictability that exemplifies competitive negotiating. This makes the car buying experience the perfect example of understanding how the effective strategic negotiator uses the techniques and predictability of competitive negotiating to manage the other negotiator's expectations and influence him to concede value.

The negotiation to purchase a car begins when a potential buyer walks into the dealership and looks at a sticker price pasted to the driver's side window. The sticker does not just provide information about the price of the car; most people know that the price on the sticker signals the beginning of a negotiation. Although some buyers simply pay the sticker price without negotiating, most do not. Instead, the seller and buyer both accept that the sticker price is the beginning of a negotiating dance. If so, why does the seller list a price on the sticker which he does not expect to be the final selling price of the car? The answer to that question has everything to do with the predictability of competitive negotiating and the management of expectations.

The dealer posts a price on the car to influence the buyer's behavior. The seller does not provide the buyer with any information about what it actually costs the manufacturer to make and market the car, or about the dealer's profit margin. Typically, the buyer does not have such information, and the dealer is not likely to share it. Still, based on experience and custom, most buyers would expect to purchase the car at a price below that advertised on the sticker. If the list price is $20,000, a buyer might conclude that $19,000 (or $18,000, or $17,000) is a good deal. The asking price, or opening offer, effectively induces the buyer to be willing to pay a higher price than if the asking price were lower. Thus, the seller's opening offer has the immediate effect of managing the buyer's expectation about the likely purchase price. This is a powerful tool that negotiators who strategically use the techniques of competitive negotiating have mastered.

The next predictable step in the car buying negotiation is for the seller to ask the buyer what he would pay to drive the car home that day. The buyer's answer to this question determines the size of the pie that must be divided—the essence of competitive bargaining. For example, if the list price is $20,000 and the buyer offers to buy the car for $16,000, the difference between the two opening offers is $4,000, which we refer to as the pie. The objective of the negotiation is to determine if the parties can agree on how to divide the $4,000 pie. The two negotiators must agree on how to divide the pie if a deal is to be reached. Either negotiator could immediately agree to the other's opening offer; the buyer could agree to the seller's offer of $20,000, or the seller could agree to the buyer's offer of $16,000. Such an outcome, however, would be unusual. The normal custom is for the seller and buyer to negotiate a way to share the $4,000 between them. That is because both are trying to maximize their shares of the pie: the seller wants to sell the car at the high-

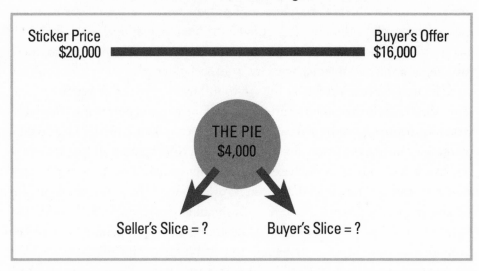

FIGURE 2-2. **The Car Purchase Negotiation: Part 1**

est price the buyer will pay, and the buyer wants to purchase the car at the lowest price the seller will accept. The parties must use the techniques of competitive negotiating to distribute the $4,000 pie between them.

Once the opening offers establish the size of the pie over which the negotiators will compete, $4,000 in this example, the next predictable step in the competitive negotiating process is that the salesperson will react in some manner to the buyer's offer to purchase the car for $16,000, not the $20,000 offered by the dealership. The salesperson could respond in different ways, but he will probably exhibit some expression of disappointment and inquire if the buyer would like to look at less expensive cars. When the buyer refuses and insists that he wants to buy the car in question for $16,000, the salesperson will relent; but he will explain that every offer, even those that he is skeptical about, must be shared with the "sales manager." Even though he is not optimistic, the salesperson will promise to do his best when presenting the buyer's offer to the sales manager. The salesperson will then leave to speak to the sales manager. The buyer waits in the salesperson's cubicle.

The salesperson returns in 10-15 minutes with renewed enthusiasm for putting this deal together. He will tell the buyer that the sales manager saw the buyer walking around the lot and thinks he looks like a nice person. The salesperson will say that the sales manager wants to do what it takes to put this nice buyer in a new car today. The sales manager has given permission to sell the car, originally priced at $20,000, for $19,000. This is a "special offer" being extended to the buyer. The sales agent will seem very pleased to have achieved such a good deal for the buyer.

The buyer will exhibit frustration and reveal a report from an online research source showing that sometimes dealers sell the model in question, with the same accessories, for $17,000. The salesperson will provide some explanation or other about why the car is being offered for $19,000, not $17,000. But then, the salesperson will ask the buyer whether he would pay $17,000. The buyer confirms that he would pay $17,000. The seller will express doubt about whether the sales manager will approve such a low price. The salesperson will confide to the buyer that the sales manager is, in fact, very tough about such things. But the salesperson will agree to fight for the buyer, and he will leave to pitch the proposal to the sales manager while the buyer remains in the cubicle.

This time the salesperson will be gone for 20-30 minutes. (Some speculate that the sales person in such situations is watching a televised basketball game or making personal calls during this interlude. Whether this is true or not probably depends on the dealership; the authors make no judgments one way or the other.) When the salesperson returns, he will have something to share confidentially with the buyer. The salesperson will explain that the dealership is going to bend the rules so that the buyer can take advantage of the manufacturer's special promotional sales price which supposedly begins next week or expired last week. With this bending of the rules, the buyer can have the car for $18,500. The salesperson will express surprise that the sales manager consented to such a sweet deal and will urge the buyer to accept it.

When the buyer says that he will never pay that kind of money for the car, the salesperson will declare that the parties are too close to not find a way to agree on a price. He will then ask if there is anything the buyer can do to sweeten the offer so the salesperson has an excuse to plead for further reductions from the sales manager. The buyer will disclose that the most he wanted

FIGURE 2-3. **The Car Purchase Negotiation: Part 2**

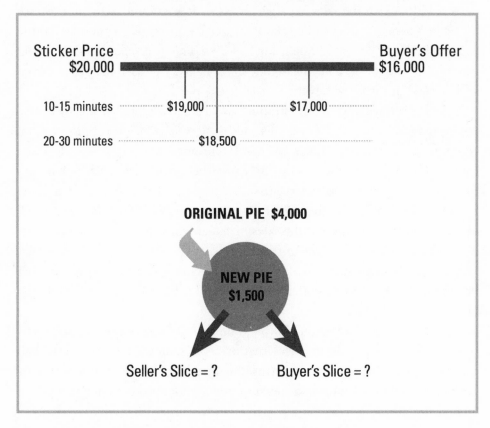

to spend was $17,500, and the salesperson will agree that is a reasonable offer. This time it will take the salesperson nearly an hour to return with a further reduction from the sales manager. The new special sales price is $18,250.

The negotiation dance continues with each side taking a step toward the other. After what is likely to be several hours, the buyer might offer $17,990 and the seller might offer $18,010. Fatigue and frustration combine to cause the buyer to declare that if the dealership will include the deluxe floor mats, he will agree to pay $18,000. Even though they are only $20 apart, the seller may well respond that it is against dealership policy to include floor mats.

FIGURE 2-4. **The Car Purchase Negotiation: Part 3**

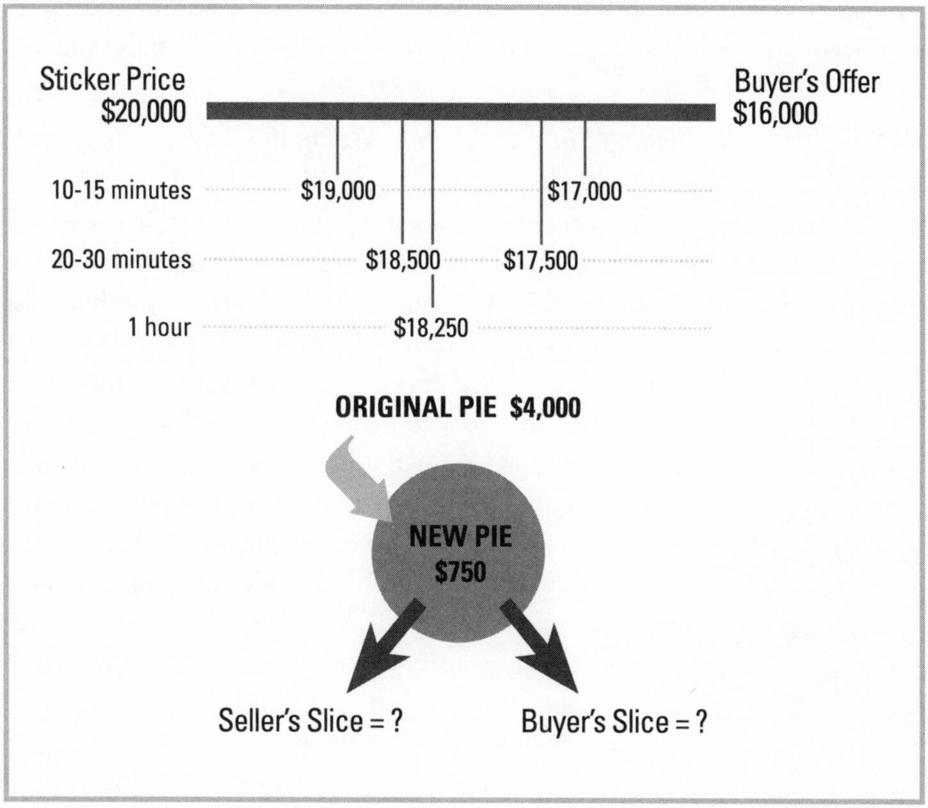

Sticker Price $20,000		Buyer's Offer $16,000
10-15 minutes	$19,000	$17,000
20-30 minutes	$18,500	$17,500
1 hour	$18,250	

ORIGINAL PIE $4,000

NEW PIE $750

Seller's Slice = ?   Buyer's Slice = ?

After investing most of the day narrowing the difference to a relatively small amount, the buyer may decide that he is so frustrated with this salesperson and the dealership that he prefers to spend money at another dealership. Alternatively, either the seller or the buyer may make the last concession and an agreement is reached. Both scenarios occur at the end of many competitive negotiations.

Strategic negotiators drive the competitive negotiation by harnessing that predictability to manage the other negotiator's expectations and induce him to concede as much of the pie as possible.

The Six Characteristics of Competitive Bargaining

The car buying experience illustrates six fundamental characteristics of competitive negotiating which every successful negotiator should understand and use.

One: Claiming the Biggest Slice of the Pie—Being the Driver, Not the Passenger

The first characteristic of competitive negotiating that the strategic negotiator must recognize is the nature of the negotiation itself: It is a competition over a fixed pie of value. The strategic negotiator has a choice about how she approaches distributing shares of the pie. Whatever approach they take, however, each negotiator must trade concessions in order to divide the pie. Of necessity, each negotiator must decide how much of the pie to give up in order to gain a certain percentage of the pie. The only way one negotiator's share of the pie gets bigger is if the other negotiator's share of the pie gets smaller. One advances only at the other's expense, but each advance comes at the expense of some share of the pie. What makes competitive negotiating so interesting and challenging is that each negotiator must consent to sacrifice a part of the pie to gain a larger share of the pie. Either both negotiators come away with equal shares of the pie, or one negotiator will come away with a larger piece. Whether you are negotiating the purchase of a new computer system for your travel agency or you are negotiating the sale of your technology company to a Fortune 500 corporation, competitive negotiating is the same: Both negotiators are trying to get the biggest slice of pie they can.

> **Negotiating Tip**
>
> To discover whether you are good or bad at competitive negotiating, analyze your most recent car buying experience: where you the driver or the passenger in that negotiation?

Two: Competitive Negotiating is Positional

A second characteristic of competitive negotiating is that the negotiators proceed from positions. The negotiation begins when an issue is identified. The issue raises a question; for example, the appropriate price for a new washing

FIGURE 2-5. **Competitive Negotiation = Positional Bargaining**

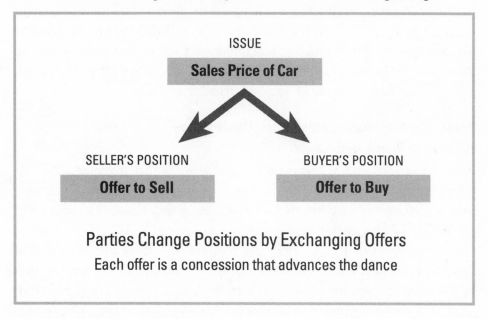

machine. One of the parties suggests an answer or solution to that issue—his position, which is expressed in the form of an offer. If the negotiation is about the sale of an appliance in a retail outlet, the retailer's listed price is the seller's position on that issue, and the consumer's offer to purchase the appliance at a lower price is the buyer's position on the same issue.

During the negotiation, both negotiators change their positions about how to divide the pie by exchanging offers in which they make concessions—giving up small slices in order to come out of the negotiation with the biggest possible slice. The competitive negotiating dance ends when both negotiators' positions are the same: They both agree on how big their respective slices of the pie will be. At that point, a deal has been reached.

As is frequently the case in competitive negotiations, whether they involve the purchase of furniture in a retail store or the sale of a fleet of delivery vans by a large dealer, the negotiators take very different positions about how to divide the pie at the beginning. The competitive negotiating dance is driven by the negotiators' willingness to change their positions by the exchange of concessions in order to reach a deal about how to divide the pie. In competitive negotiating, the negotiators communicate their positions about how to divide the pie through the offers they make. The offers do all the talking, and, as we will explain below, much can be learned from them.

Three: The Negotiators Must Make Concessions in Order to Reach Agreement

A third characteristic of competitive negotiating is that it requires concessions by each negotiator in order for an agreement to be reached. A concession is a change in one negotiator's position in order to induce the other negotiator to change his position. Concessions are a shift from a more extreme position to a more moderate position, or giving up something of value to get something of value. The computer retailer makes a concession by discounting a popular personal computer system from its suggested retail price. The consumer makes a concession when she increases her offer to purchase the system in response to the discount offer by the seller. Concession is just another word for compromise. Concessions or compromises are the lifeblood of competitive negotiating, the music to which the negotiators dance. When the negotiators stop making concessions, the music ceases, and the dance comes to an end.

Four: There is a Pattern to the Timing and Size of Concessions

A fourth and important characteristic of competitive negotiating is that there is a pattern to both the size and timing of concessions. This is the language by which competitive negotiators signal their degree of flexibility in their positions; that communication can either be strategic or unintentional. Usually, strategic negotiators start the competitive negotiating dance with larger concessions that get smaller as the negotiation proceeds. Often, the size of each subsequent concession is approximately half the size of the prior concession. Thus, with each concession, the negotiator not only gives up something of value, but the size of the concession signals whether the negotiator has more or less flexibility. This simple rule enables the strategic negotiator to give up less and gain more in competitive negotiating.

While the size of a concession sends an important signal about a negotiator's degree of flexibility, the amount of time in which the concession is made is equally significant. A quick concession gives the impression that it was effortless, suggesting that additional concessions are readily available. Conversely, if a concession takes longer to make, the negotiator signals less flexibility and that future concessions are likely to be smaller. Strategic negotiators use the timing and size of concessions together to signal less flexibility when it is useful to do so. This, in turn, manages the expectations of the other negotiator so that he will not expect easy or sizeable concessions as the negotiation progresses. Managing the other negotiator's expectations in this way may motivate him to make more concessions. Thus, you can minimize the concessions you make and maximize the concessions the other negotiator makes, which makes for a bigger slice of pie for you!

This principle is illustrated by the automobile sale negotiation discussed earlier. It also occurs in many other competitive negotiations all the time. For example, consider a negotiation for the sale of goods, lumber for example. The buyer inquires whether the seller will offer a discount if the buyer purchases a certain volume of lumber of a specific cut, type, and grade of wood. If the seller promptly concedes a discount, for example 20%, the buyer perceives that the seller is very flexible about the price because a sizeable concession occurred quickly. If the buyer is a strategic negotiator, he might offer to purchase the goods for a 40% discount, hoping to negotiate a discount of 25-30%. A big concession which occurs quickly sends a clear signal of flexibility to the other negotiator. If you are desperate to sell your inventory, perhaps doing this is okay. More often than not, however, such large and quick concessions unnecessarily concede too much of the pie.

If the seller wishes to signal a willingness to discount the goods, but a lack of flexibility about the size of the discount, she will respond differently. Instead of quickly conceding such a sizeable discount, the strategic negotiator will manage the buyer's expectation by taking longer to offer a smaller discount. For example, the buyer may ask whether the seller is offering a "good price" on a certain volume of the lumber. The seller may say something, "Well, that type and grade is in high demand, and my supplier does not cut me any sweet deals on it, but I'll see what we can do for you. You're a good customer, and I want to take care of you." The seller might turn to the side and make some entries on a calculator. The seller may say she needs to check with someone else to see if such a discount is available. She may leave to "make a phone call" or to "check the computer" or some such. This communicates that the discount is difficult to make, thus creating the impression that any concession she makes will not be followed by further concessions. After this bit of play-acting, the seller might offer a 10% discount along with language indicating that this is a very good deal for a good customer. "Well, we were able to work the numbers and offer you 10% off if you purchase 1,000 units, cash, today. That's a great price." These and similar comments are common in such situations. Regardless of the words you use, the message is the same: The timing and size of the concession have signaled that the buyer is not going to get as big a slice of the pie as she may have anticipated.

Making and responding to offers in a way that manages the other negotiator's expectations can take between three minutes and a number of days. Even a three-minute pause can create the perception to the buyer that a discount is difficult. A three-day delay in responding to the proposal makes that message even firmer: The concession is difficult to make, so it might not be granted, or, if it is, more concessions should not be expected. The buyer who needs the product will be less likely to kill the deal by seeking further concessions as a result of the seller's management of the timing and size of his concession. The seller has effectively managed the buyer's expectation of the likely sales price and encouraged the buyer to pay more by manipulating the timing and size of the concession.

Some commentators have suggested that, in pure competitive negotiating, each successive concession is half the size of the one before it and takes twice as long to achieve. In the car buying experience discussed above, the salesperson takes 10-15 minutes in which to respond to the buyer's first offer. After the buyer's second offer, the salesperson is gone for 20-30 minutes—twice as long. The third time he might be gone closer to an hour. This doubling of the time between progressively smaller concessions is not acciden-tal, but it is strategically calculated to manage the buyer's expectation about the seller's flexibility and willingness to make concessions. This strategy is remarkably effective for car dealerships: They consistently maximize their return, that is, their slice of the pie. Effective strategic negotiators reap the same success by using this funda-mental technique of competitive negotiating. This is how they become drivers of the competitive negotiation.

> ### Negotiating Tip
>
> A good competitive negotia-tor manages the other negotiator's expectations by strategically manipulating the timing and size of concessions.

For small businesses, mastering the timing and size of concessions is the difference between a fat profit margin and a slim one. The reason for this is simple: In the busi-ness world, if you do not strategically manage the timing and size of conces-sions to manipulate the other negotiator's expectations, the other negotiator may do it to you.

Even though it is an effective way of maximizing value, competitive nego-tiating can also create tension and anxiety in those who are uncomfortable with this approach. The combination of each successive concession being about half the size of the previous concession and taking twice as long to accomplish creates frustration for many about the efficiency of this approach, especially in the later stages. For example, expending two hours in the car dealership to resolve the last $100 of the deal is frustrating to many people. Those who react this way typically view the experience as gamesmanship, and it is. The problem is that if one negotiator is good at this game, and the other is not, the former is likely to get a better deal than the latter. So it pays to understand this game and be good at it. Competition is not a dirty word in the business world; it is the key to profit or loss for all businesses large and small. Being competitive means mastering the manipulation that is at the heart of competitive negotiating so that you can compete effectively, whether you are purchasing inventory or selling products to the customer. And while we will discuss later how to not let the gamesmanship of competitive negotiating get out of hand, most small businesses are not effective competitive negotiators. We would like to see that situation change.

Five: The End-Point Is Likely to be the Mid-Point Between the First Two Reasonable Offers

A fifth characteristic of competitive bargaining is that, if an agreement is reached, the end-point likely will be at or near the mid-point between the first two reasonable offers. This makes sense. If the parties are both competitive and have submitted reasonable proposals, their exchange of concessions is likely to take them very close to the mid-point between those starting points. This description of the likely result of competitive negotiating assumes negotiators of roughly equivalent bargaining power and the exchange of reciprocal concessions. Not all competitive negotiations are like that. Still, many commentators have observed this characteristic of competitive negotiating to be true as a general principle. There is a psychological reason why competitive negotiating frequently results in an agreement at or near the mid-point between the first two reasonable offers: Bad feelings between the negotiators are avoided if they both perceive they are equally sharing the burden of creating the deal. Both parties save face by an even compromise.

> ### Negotiating Tip
>
> When negotiating competitively, plan your moves based upon the likely end-point of the dance.

It is important to note that the likely end-point in a competitive negotiation is not the mid-point between the first two offers regardless of their reasonableness. The end-point is likely to be the mid-point between the first two *reasonable* offers. For example, in the sale of a new plasma television at a retail outlet, in response to a sticker price of $6,000, the buyer might offer $500. The mid point between $500 and $6,000 is $3,250. The seller is not likely to sell the TV at that price. An offer of $4,000 from the buyer, on the other hand, may be a reasonable offer. The mid-point between $4,000 and $6,000 is $5,000, a probable ending point of the competitive negotiating dance for the purchase of the television, depending on the market. When either or both of the negotiators make unreasonable opening offers, the end-point likely will not be the mid-point between those two proposals. Instead, once the negotiators have made offers within the reasonable range, the end-point likely will be the mid-point between those two proposals.

The strategic negotiator uses the predictability of the likely ending point of the negotiation, along with the timing and size of the concessions, to make an opening or responding offer which drives the negotiation to the ending point the negotiator desires. Thus, the seller of the television makes an opening offer of $6,000, hoping to sell it for $5,000, $5,500, or maybe even $6,000, again depending on the market and the seller's cost. The buyer makes a responding offer of $4,000, hoping to purchase the television for $5,000, $4,500, or maybe even $4,000. Each negotiator is trying for the ending point which splits the pie the most in his or her favor.

Six: A Negotiator Short Circuits the Dance at Her Own Risk

A sixth characteristic of competitive negotiating is that one should not short circuit the dance. Assume that the car purchase negotiation described earlier in this chapter concludes with an agreement that the buyer will buy the car for $18,000. Also assume that this buyer is your neighbor. The next day she takes you on a drive in her new car and tells you the purchase price. You decide that you want to buy the same car for the same price. Your neighbor tells you the dealership and salesperson from whom she bought the car. You immediately go to the same dealership and ask for the same salesperson. You explain that you are the neighbor of the person who bought the car yesterday and that you want the same car at the same price.

If the salesperson and dealership are cooperative negotiators, they will accept your offer and conclude business quickly. But that is not what happens on this planet. Automobile dealerships, like most businesses, are likely to perceive your reasonable opening offer as an indication that you might pay more than your neighbor. The dealership will find some way to distinguish the car it sold to your neighbor yesterday from the cars currently available (for example, the length of time in inventory or manufacturer incentives or options). From the dealership's perspective, there is a $2,000 pie (the difference between the asking price of $20,000 and your opening offer of $18,000). The dealership will try to get as much of that $2,000 as it can get. Thus, the negotiator who tries to save time and frustration by short-circuiting the dance simply experiences more frustration when the competitive negotiator tries to claim a slice of the newly-defined pie.

The Culture of Competitive Negotiating

If you do not like the competitive negotiating dance and are inclined to cut it short, think about situations in which you might view competitive negotiating as a natural and expected process. The dance is a ritual in which both negotiators either claim or concede value. The strategic negotiator has the power of choosing whether he is giving up or gaining value in that negotiation. In American culture, we expect the dance when buying cars or homes, when we are at flea markets and garage sales, or maybe even when we purchase furniture or appliances. In those contexts, you do what is customary and expected: barter for the best price. This is true in other cultures as well. So long as both negotiators have the same expectation about the process of their negotiation, the dance is expected and likely to produce agreement. If the competitive negotiating dance is customary and appropriate, you have the power to manage that process in a way that maximizes your slice of the pie. That is what strategic negotiators do.

Culture also plays another role in the competitive negotiating dance. In some cultures, negotiators love a good, long dance. In others, negotiators do not like to dance at all. In the United States, the cultural norm disfavors competitive negotiating, except in the automobile, home, flea market, and commercial contexts described above. The average number of moves most Americans make in the competitive bargaining dance ranges from one to three, while in many other cultures the norm is from five to ten, sometimes even more. And it is not surprising that Americans do not do this dance much.

Apart from the above exceptions, most commercial transactions in the United States with which people are most familiar, including shopping at grocery and department stores, do not involve haggling at all. Haggling at the grocery store is unheard of, so a store clerk would be mystified about how to respond to a customer's offer of $1.50 for a can of soup marked $2.95. In this situation, both negotiators would not be on the same page—one expects to dance and the other is not accustomed to doing so.

In our culture, we experience competitive negotiating or haggling usually when we buy cars or houses. Since the average American buys a car only every two to ten years and a house only every five to twenty years, he or she has very little practice in or patience with the competitive negotiating dance and tends to dislike it. It is hard to learn to do something you have not been taught, that you do not practice, and that you do not like. It is no wonder why you are reading this book!

Competitive negotiating skills, such as strategically managing the timing and size of concessions, or not short-circuiting the dance, can be learned and practiced. Our attitudes can change to actually embrace and revel in the opportunity to dance. Many of us already enjoy the dance in certain situations. When the average American vacations out of the country, he often finds himself in a culture that expects the tourist to haggle for souvenirs. In these situations, we have permission to haggle, and we find it exhilarating and entertaining. Sometimes, we haggle at foreign markets for trinkets we might not even need or want! Haggling in these situations is okay, so we do it. Think of the last time you brought home something for which you haggled while on vacation, and you were greeted with the question, "What were you thinking when you bought this?" Your answer? "But I got such a great deal on it!" The fact is that we enjoyed getting the vendor to greatly reduce her price. We felt competent, victorious!

If we travel thousands of miles to have these experiences, what stops us from engaging in the same competitive negotiating dance here at home? Nothing, except our personalities, background, and experiences. If we can enjoy the competitive dance when we give ourselves permission to do so abroad, we should consider giving ourselves permission to do the same dance here, in our businesses and in our lives. The profitability of your business depends on minimizing operating expenses and maximizing revenue. You can do that by mastering the competitive negotiating dance. If you are not good at competitive negotiating, then you are not managing your business as you should. But before you get stressed out about becoming a better competitive negotiator, think about the last time you enjoyed haggling while on vacation. If you enjoyed it then, you can learn to enjoy it as an integral part of managing your business.

> **Negotiating Tip**
>
> The strategic negotiator is the choreographer of a well-managed dance in which the result is predictable from the opening moves.

The next time a customer asks for a discount, picture yourself at that bazaar in Mexico, or Costa Rica, or Istanbul, or Hong Kong. Like the merchant from whom you bought that beautiful trinket, the customer likely will not resent the dance at all. Instead, the customer may feel that she got a great deal because you reduced the price in slower, smaller increments. In reality, you also will have gained what you needed: a sale at the best price possible. When both sides get what they need for a price with which they are satisfied, the result is a great deal. The seller and buyer get what they need in a well-managed commercial transaction, and this is what being in business is all about.

The Opening Offer: The Strategic Negotiator's First Major Decision

Strategic negotiators know that the opening offer presents an important and powerful opportunity to manage the other negotiator's expectations. The authors regularly ask groups of students studying negotiation to pair off and negotiate a simulated sale of goods. What the students do not know is that they have a large zone of agreement built into their negotiation. In other words, the seller and buyer are both willing to compromise a great deal to reach agreement, but neither negotiator knows how much room the other has to move. Thus, the negotiators in this exercise have a large dance floor ready for them to claim value by using the techniques of competitive negotiating discussed

FIGURE 2-6. **Purchase/Sale Transaction: Part One**

above. All the students representing the seller have identical instructions about their negotiating flexibility. All the students playing the buyers have identical instructions about their negotiating flexibility. You might expect that the deals reached by the students would be very similar, but the results are surprising.

Out of twenty pairs of negotiators, inevitably several of the groups reach agreements in which either the buyer is paying substantially more than the buyers in other groups or the seller is selling for substantially less than the sellers in other groups. When the results from all the groups are written on the board in front of the class, the buyers who paid substantially more than the others or the sellers who sold for substantially less than the others are surprised or embarrassed. The different deals reached by the negotiators, all of whom had the same set of buyer's or seller's facts, usually look something like the chart in Figure 2-7.

In each instance in which a negotiator in this exercise gets an exceptionally good result and the other negotiator agrees to an exceptionally poor deal,

FIGURE 2-7. **Purchase/Sale Transaction: Part Two**

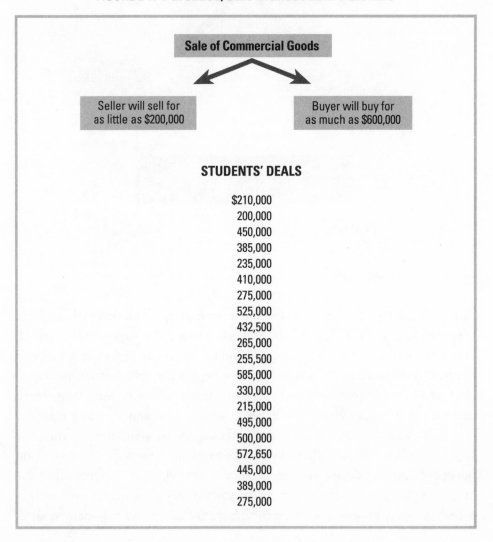

Sale of Commercial Goods

Seller will sell for as little as $200,000

Buyer will buy for as much as $600,000

STUDENTS' DEALS

$210,000
200,000
450,000
385,000
235,000
410,000
275,000
525,000
432,500
265,000
255,500
585,000
330,000
215,000
495,000
500,000
572,650
445,000
389,000
275,000

there is a common explanation: The negotiator who did well made a strong opening offer that effectively managed the other negotiator's expectations. When we list the opening offers on the board, it usually looks something like the list shown in Figure 2-8. There is a clear pattern that explains these

FIGURE 2-8. **Purchase/Sale Transaction: Part Three**

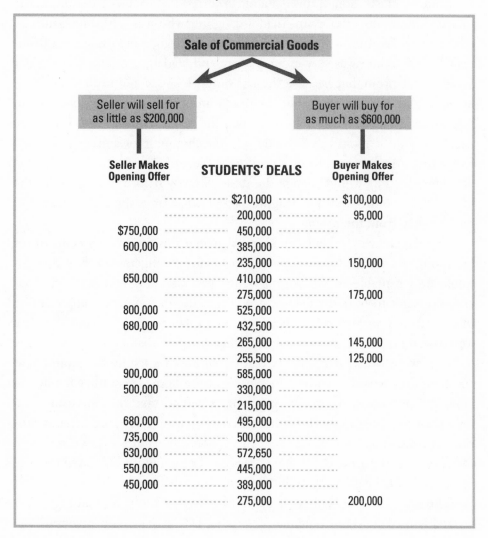

Seller Makes Opening Offer	STUDENTS' DEALS	Buyer Makes Opening Offer
	$210,000	$100,000
	200,000	95,000
$750,000	450,000	
600,000	385,000	
	235,000	150,000
650,000	410,000	
	275,000	175,000
800,000	525,000	
680,000	432,500	
	265,000	145,000
	255,500	125,000
900,000	585,000	
500,000	330,000	
	215,000	
680,000	495,000	
735,000	500,000	
630,000	572,650	
550,000	445,000	
450,000	389,000	
	275,000	200,000

results. When the buyer opened low, the sales price was lower. When the seller opened high, the sales price was higher. This illustrates a fundamental truth about competitive negotiating: You can get more or less depending on what your opening offer is. It sounds so simple, but, in practice, negotiators ignore this powerful truth every day. Effective strategic negotiators do not; they are masters of the power of the opening offer.

Another illustration of this dynamic occurred in a friend's parenting experience. The friend—the mom—had a daughter who was a freshman in high school. The daughter was invited to the Senior Prom, a big thing for a freshman. The daughter was very excited. Mom and Dad agreed that the daughter could go the prom, but because she was only 14, she would need to be home by midnight. Mom wanted to be the one to inform the daughter and tried to discuss the curfew in the weeks preceding the prom. During that period, the daughter and the mom had a wonderful time shopping for a dress and shoes. Every time Mom started to bring up the subject of the curfew, however, the daughter skillfully would change the topic. Shortly before the big night, the mom finally confronted her daughter about what time she was expected to return home from the prom.

The daughter explained that she anticipated this might be a concern for the mom, but that she and her date had made arrangements they thought would be acceptable and reassuring to the parents. The mom was delighted and was eager to hear the details, proud that her daughter was approaching this discussion so maturely. The daughter explained that she and her date would share a limousine with three other couples that evening. After the prom, they all would attend a party at the home of a family the mom knew, and then they would attend another party at the home of another family the mom did not know. Then, the group intended to take the limousine to a restaurant that over looks the ocean where they would have breakfast at sunrise. The daughter emphasized that there would be adults at the after-prom parties, and that no alcohol would be served. The daughter estimated that she would be home by about 9:00 the morning after the prom.

The mom could not believe her ears. She also was both hurt and angry. She reacted immediately and vehemently. "Young lady, that's totally unacceptable.

What were you thinking? The answer is no, absolutely not. You are to be home not a second later than 2:00 A.M., is that clear?" With that, the mom left the room. As she walked away to regroup, she suddenly was in shock. She could not believe that she had agreed to 2:00 A.M. She and her husband had agreed that the curfew should be midnight. How could this have happened?

The mom, who is a successful business professional, shared this story with the authors because she realized that her expectations had been managed skillfully by her daughter. A curfew of 2:00 A.M. seemed like a giant victory compared to her daughter's opening offer of 9:00 A.M. We refer to this power of the opening offer as "the magnetic pull effect." The mom confirmed her theory when she later saw an e-mail on the family computer in which the daughter had written to a friend, "I did pretty good. I got until 2:00. How did you do?" Kudos to the daughter for her negotiation instincts, but we must question her judgment in leaving such incriminating evidence on the family computer. That unwise move aside, the daughter did what strategic negotiators do to get better deals: She managed her mom's expectations by making an opening offer which induced the mom to revise her previous curfew to a time closer to the daughter's proposal. If you have children, this probably has happened to you in one way or another more than once. Children are born negotiators!

The strategic negotiator understands that the magnetic pull effect of the opening offer has a way of shaping the outcome of the negotiation from its very first round. In order to make effective use of this power, and to avoid having his own expectations managed by the other negotiator's opening offer, the strategic negotiator should assess the following three factors: 1) Who opens; 2) what the opening offer should be; and 3) how the opening offer should be phrased.

Who Opens

The strategic negotiator's first important decision is whether to make the opening offer or to let the other negotiator do so. Many of the students in our negotiation skills courses assume that it is always best to let the other negotiator make the opening offer. In some instances, in personal injury claims, for example, insurance adjusters have a custom of insisting on the injured person making the opening offer. There are advantages to letting the other negotiator make the first offer. The negotiator who receives the opening offer learns two kinds of information: First, how does the other side value the thing being negotiated, whether it is a good, a service, or property? Second, how does the other party negotiate? This is important information to the strategic negotiator, who shapes his or her moves accordingly.

Letting the other negotiator make the opening offer also has disadvantages. Remember that the first offer on the table has the greatest opportunity to manage the recipient's expectations. By letting the other negotiator make the first offer, we are allowing ourselves to become vulnerable to being managed. If we are thinking strategically, would we rather manage the expectations of the other negotiator or have the other negotiator manage our expectations? When the issue is framed this way, most people agree that it is usually better for us to manage the other negotiator's expectations. If you are in a position of leverage, for example, or if you have readily available alternatives to reaching a deal in the negotiation, you may wish to make the opening offer because of its power to influence the other negotiator's expectations. You can shape the deal to your liking at the outset by using the magnetic pull effect of the opening offer.

In the business world, common examples of using the magnetic pull effect of the opening offer include the Manufacturer's Suggested Retail Price ("MSRP") sticker on automobiles or appliances, an offer of employment with a specific compensation package, or an advertised price for goods or products. Examples of instances in which it can be good for the business negotiator to let the other negotiator make the opening offer include employment negotiations, negotiations for the purchase of a business, and negotiations for the purchase of equipment or supplies.

What the Opening Offer Should Be

The negotiator who chooses to make an opening offer then must decide what to do. Should the opening offer be extreme or reasonable? Should we ask for more or less? What reaction do we expect the opening offer to engender? Is that a result we wish to encourage or discourage? These questions hint at the strategic significance of the opening offer. If we ask for too little, we will not have claimed all the value we might. If we ask for too much, we might discourage the other negotiator from continuing the negotiation, or she might react strongly and offer too little to justify further compromise. The importance of the opening offer is magnified depending upon whether we are innately cooperative or competitive. The naturally cooperative negotiator tends to make opening offers which are reasonable from his perspective, but which do not aim for enough value. The naturally competitive negotiator tends to make opening offers which more cooperative negotiators view as "extreme." Sometimes extreme offers succeed in maximizing value, and other times they kill deals.

The effective strategic negotiator is thoughtful about balancing the mixed motives of competition and cooperation in the opening offer. The choices available to the negotiator in making an opening offer can be summarized on a continuum between reasonable and extreme proposals. A reasonable offer is one that the negotiator believes could be within the other negotiator's range of acceptable outcomes. There are instances in which a reasonable opening offer makes good strategic sense. For example, if a seller knows a potential buyer has other readily available sources of the good or service being negotiated, the seller may wish to make an opening offer that is comparable to the other deals the buyer could make. That would be a reasonable opening offer. A reasonable opening offer is also strategically advantageous when the negotiator has an ongoing business or negotiating relationship with the other negotiator. A reasonable opening offer is more credible than an extreme proposal in this situation. Otherwise, being too competitive may undermine the cooperation necessary to continuing the mutually beneficial relationship.

An extreme opening offer is one that the negotiator believes is outside the other negotiator's range of acceptable outcomes. This negotiator is trying to manage the other negotiator's expectations in order to induce him or her to make as many concessions as possible. The essence of competitive negotiating is to maximize value by encouraging the other negotiator to make such com-

promises. Extreme opening offers are a certain way to motivate the other negotiator to agree to a deal which is at the furthest end of the range of his acceptable outcomes. Reasonable opening offers do not have that effect. Also, an
extreme opening offer creates a larger dance floor, which permits the strategic
negotiator plenty of room to dance, that is, make concessions. In the student
exercise discussed previously, the sellers who got the highest price for the
inventory they were selling made extreme opening offers. The buyers who got
the lowest price made extremely low opening offers. The results these negotiators achieved were not accidental: Extreme opening offers manage expectations and frequently get the strategic negotiator a bigger slice of the pie.

The problem with extreme opening offers is that they can backfire if they
are too extreme. An extreme opening offer runs the risk of being perceived by
the other negotiator as insulting or offensive. This, in turn, can motivate the
other negotiator to turn off or respond in an insulting or offensive manner
which does not further the negotiation. The point of a well-managed extreme
opening offer is to encourage concessions from the other negotiator, not drive
him or her from the table. Therefore, the strategic negotiator fashions the
extreme opening offer in a manner so that it is just credible enough to encourage significant concessions from the other negotiator. For example, when
negotiating the amount per square foot on a lease, the lessee may start by saying what he is paying now (even though he has been in a long-term lease and
he knows rates have increased), or the amount another potential landlord
quoted (even though that property is in a less desirable location). These opening offers may be extreme in relation to what the landlord will accept, but they
are linked to a plausible standard—what the tenant is currently paying or can
get with another landlord. The point of the extreme opening offer is to maximize value but to keep the other negotiator at the table.

The Phrasing of the Opening Offer

Whether you make an extreme or a reasonable opening offer, you must pay
careful attention to the language that attends the proposal. The danger of a
reasonable opening offer is that it may signal flexibility the negotiator making
the offer does not have. The challenge of the extreme opening offer is that it

FIGURE 2-9. **Strategic Choices for the Opening Offer**

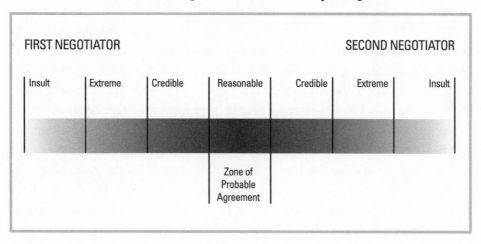

might be viewed by the recipient as too unreasonable and insulting, thus killing the negotiation. Therefore, the strategic negotiator has to decide what language should be used in delivering the opening offer. The words he chooses send a signal to the other negotiator. The question is what signal should the negotiator send? Here are some guidelines for phrasing opening offers.

Reasonable Opening Offer = Firm Language

When you make a reasonable opening offer, it is best to phrase it in words that communicate firmness and little, if any, flexibility. The following are examples of firm opening offer language:

"*I cannot sell this for less than …*"

"*We have done a lot of research, and we cannot justify a price higher than …*"

"*This is my best and only offer. It's nonnegotiable.*"

"*We will not pay more than $X.*"

"*If we go back and forth, this is the last step in the dance, and it's the best I can do.*"

"*For these reasons, this is a fair proposal, and while I am willing to work with you to put together a deal, I have very little room to move.*"

Caveat: The danger of reasonable and firm opening offers is that the negotiator takes the risk that the other negotiator will perceive the offer as the beginning of a process in which both sides are expected to compromise. The reasonable and firm offer is an attempt to short circuit the dance. Even after assuring the other negotiator the offer is firm and there is little room for concessions, the negotiator who makes a reasonable and firm opening offer unintentionally may invite an extreme counter offer from the other negotiator who expects to go through the ritual of the negotiating dance. Thus, reasonable opening offers should only be made when the negotiator knows the other negotiator and anticipates a reasonable response, or when the negotiator is in a particularly strong position and can walk away if the other negotiator responds with an extreme counter-offer. It may be hard for the other negotiator who responds extremely to a reasonable opening offer to make the concessions necessary to reach agreement. Such lopsided movement in a negotiation results in a serious loss of face, which most negotiators will not accept unless they have no other choice than to continue bidding against themselves.

Reasonable Offers Should Be Preceded by the Reasoning Supporting Them

Too often, negotiators present their proposals without explaining the justification for them. Strategic negotiators understand, however, that saying the number first means that the other negotiator will not be listening when the explanation follows. Instead, effective negotiators provide the reasoning in support of the offer first, so that the proposal seems more reasonable. This approach, when linked with firm language, makes the reasonable opening offer more credible. Only when the firm language attending the reasonable opening offer is credible will the other negotiator's reaction be effectively managed.

Extreme Opening Offer = Soft Language

In contrast to the reasonable and firm opening offer, the extreme offer must be presented softly; that is, with language signaling flexibility. The softness in the presentation allows the negotiator to make concessions without losing credibility. This is important: An extreme, but firm opening offer will be met with skepticism in two ways. First, the other negotiator may perceive that your opening offer is so unrealistic that you must not know what you are doing, which means you have no credibility and can be exploited. Second, the other negotiator may take your extreme but firm opening offer seriously and conclude that he will not be able to do the deal with you. Either result is counter-productive if you wish to maximize value and reach agreement. Examples of soft opening qualifiers include:

> *"My client/boss believes the price should be $X."*
>
> *"I sold/bought a ___ like this last week for $X ."*
>
> *"What do you think about $X?"*
>
> *"With the information I have now, I would offer you $X."*
>
> *"We are looking to sell/buy for something in the neighborhood of $Y."*

Caveat: The language you use to communicate flexibility in an extreme opening offer should not be too soft. For example, it would not be wise to say, "I will open/start the negotiation at $X" or "I will offer $X, but it is negotiable." These are poorly worded opening offers because they signal too much flexibility. Such wording encourages an extreme response from the other negotiator. This is a mismanagement of expectations. Whenever you see a real estate advertisement which says, "Offered at . . ." or "Asking . . .," this signals so much flexibility that in most instances the benefit of an extreme opening offer is lost. If the seller desperately needs to sell, perhaps such soft language may be appropriate, but it is never a wise choice to signal desperation at the beginning of any negotiation. Well-worded extreme openings maximize the value available in the negotiation by signaling just enough firmness to be taken seriously, while at the same time signaling just enough flexibility to keep the other negotiator at the table.

The strategic negotiator approaches each negotiation with answers to the following questions:

- Am I going to make the opening offer, or am I going to let the other negotiator do so?

> ## Negotiating Tip
>
> Effective strategic negotiators use the power of the opening offer to shape the negotiation to end at their preferred agreement point: determining the destination from the opening offer.

- If I am going to make the opening offer, do I want it to be extreme or reasonable?
- If I make an extreme opening offer, what language should I choose that will signal just enough flexibility to invite a substantial concession from the other negotiator?
- If I make a reasonable opening offer, what language should I choose that will signal to the other negotiator that I have very little room to move?
- Whatever opening offer strategy I employ, what do I expect the other negotiator to do?
- What is my plan if the other negotiator responds with a reasonable counter-offer?
- What is my plan if the other negotiator responds with an extreme counter-offer?
- Do I need this deal? If so, how badly?

Rather than resenting or fearing this dance, the negotiator should embrace the empowerment that comes with it. Armed with a strategy for maximizing value, building your dance floor and managing the other negotiator's expectations, you are in control of the negotiation. Fear of competitive negotiating stems from lack of confidence and control over the process. Understanding the dynamics of this ritual, however, makes it fun. The best negotiators drive their way to better deals, and you can do it, too.

Linkage: Connecting Different Pies to Create Deals

There are times when the negotiators have a hard time reaching agreement on how to distribute value within a specific fixed pie. For example, the parties in a real estate transaction may have done the competitive negotiating dance for several moves, but cannot agree on price. The buyer and seller are $500 apart. If they both need to consummate the sale, the buyer might suggest that the seller pay $500 worth of closing costs which would ordinarily be borne by the buyer. This attempt to connect a different pie of value to bridge a gap in another pie of value is called "linkage." Negotiators use it all the time to close deals.

Examples include escrow period, payment terms (installments, balloons, down payments), interest rate, cash versus property, collateral, and the list goes on.

Linkage can be an effective way of both maximizing value and being exploited. For example, suppose you are driving down the road one day dreaming of that luxury car you have always wanted. The only problem is that you will never be able to shell out the $80,000 necessary to purchase such a car. Suddenly, you hear on the radio, "Own the brand new Centurion for only $19.99 per month. That's right, for only $19.99 per month, we can put you into the brand new Centurion. Hurry down to Luxurio Motors today for this exceptional value." Your prayers have been answered. You resolve to go to that dealership when you get off work.

When you get to Luxurio Motors, you ask the handsomely coiffed sales associate about the $19.99 per month deal you heard advertised. He tells you it is true, you can buy the brand new Centurion for only $19.99. You ask about the other terms. Certainly, he responds. You must make a down payment of $10,000, the interest rate on the loan is 20 percent, and you will be making payments for the rest of your life! The diagram in Figure 2-10 illustrates this comedic yet useful example of linkage. The negotiation could have been about the sales price of the car. But, for the buyer in the above example, that negotiation would not have produced agreement: He could not afford this car but

FIGURE 2-10. **Linkage**

Monthly Payment $19.99	Interest Rate 20%
Down Payment $10,000	Payments the Rest of Your Life

for such a low monthly payment. So, the seller found a way to connect other pies of value to the negotiation in order to create a deal that works for the buyer. The seller offered an attractive monthly payment amount that just about anyone could meet. To compensate for such a generous term, the seller linked a high interest rate, a sizeable down payment, and a long loan period to the pie being negotiated. The buyer drives away in a car he loves and could not afford otherwise, and the seller makes a very profitable sale. Both negotiators are happy, right?

> **Definition**
>
> Linkage means connecting pies to create a deal.

The same example of linkage demonstrates its pitfalls. The seller used linkage to give the buyer a sizable benefit—a low monthly payment—but at an unconscionable price. The resulting deal is a windfall for the seller and a financially irresponsible decision for the buyer. Linkage can be a useful technique for closing deals, but it can also result in terribly bad deals for the unwitting. The key is understanding the benefits and costs of linkage so that you can make informed and responsible decisions. Otherwise, linkage can be used to exploit the other negotiator, like a carnival or street corner shell game. Anyone who has ever negotiated an automobile lease knows just how challenging it is to determine whether linkage is working for or against you.

Anchoring: The Power of Psychology

Finally, no discussion of competitive negotiating would be complete without mention of the concept of anchoring. Words are very powerful. Advertisers have long understood their power to influence the behavior of people, whether they are consumers or voters. A single concept can be received in different ways by the same listener, depending on the words chosen by the speaker. Some words create positive psychological responses, such as affection, laughter, enjoyment, or interest. Other words create negative psychological responses, such as anger, distrust, fear, or rejection. For the strategic negotiator, there is both opportunity and risk in the use of language during a negotiation.

Anchoring is a technique in which a proposal, typically a final offer, is phrased in words that encourage risk avoidance. When the recipient of an offer perceives it as being a net gain, she is more likely to avoid risk and accept the proposal. If an offer is phrased in a way that causes the other negotiator to perceive that it is a net loss, then she will be more risk tolerant and reject the offer. The strategic negotiator understands and uses the psychology of anchoring to close deals. The uninformed negotiator does not, and may phrase a final offer as a net loss for the other negotiator, thereby ending the negotiation without reaching a deal.

For an example of both negative and positive anchoring, picture a negotiation between an American power tool manufacturer with 1,000 employees and the employees' union. The employees currently are paid $7.25 per hour. They have not had a raise in five years. The union wants to increase their hourly wage considerably to be comparable with workers in other power tool factories and to compensate for the rate of inflation. Accordingly, management begins the negotiation with an opening offer of the status quo—$7.25 per hour. Management justifies the proposal with soft but principled language to the effect that competition from power tool manufacturers in China and Vietnam is pushing down prices and profits, making any substantial pay raise difficult. The union responds with an extreme opening offer of $14.00 per hour, citing the hourly wages of workers in similar power tool manufacturing plants, the rate of inflation, and the workers' investment in the well-being of the company reflected by no pay raise in five years.

The parties settle into the familiar rhythm of competitive negotiating. After many moves back and forth over the course of several days, management has reached a point when it can only make one final offer. At this point, management has offered $10.00 per hour, and the union countered at $11.25 per hour. Management can make only one more move. The company can afford to pay no more than $10.25 per hour. That is a dollar less than the union's last proposal.

At this crucial point in the negotiation, management has a choice of how to phrase its final offer. Management could present it this way: "We've been working hard to find an hourly rate upon which the company and the employees can agree. We've come a long way, but the company simply cannot afford to pay the employees $11.25 per hour. Therefore, the farthest the company can go, and our last, best and final offer is $10.25 per hour. That's $1.00 per hour less than you want, but it's the best we can do."

What reaction would this likely engender in the union negotiators? Risk tolerance: The proposal is phrased in a way which depicts acceptance of it as a net loss for the employees. Thus, phrasing the last offer in this manner runs a high risk of encouraging the union to decline the proposal and hold out for another concession. The problem is that management cannot make another concession. No deal is reached, the union goes on strike, and both the company and its employees suffer the consequences.

There is another way to make this final offer. The management negotiator might say, "Well, we have come a long way in this negotiation. We've worked hard, and I know that tough choices were made by both sides. We all want this to work. Management came into this negotiation expecting that it would only increase the hourly wage up to $9.00 per hour. But we have done more than that, far more than we planned on doing. We are prepared to make one, final proposal of a pay increase to $10.25 per hour. This reflects an increase of approximately 30 percent, which is substantially greater than the rate of inflation. This is a significant pay increase. Any more than that risks the health of the company and the jobs of the employees. We urge the employees to accept it."

Phrasing the final offer in this manner encourages risk avoidance by emphasizing the truth: The proposal is a substantial gain that would be lost if it is not accepted. Thus, the management negotiator anchors the union negotiator to gain, which, in turn, may influence the union negotiator to avoid risking that gain by demanding further concessions that might kill the deal. Anchoring is a powerful technique strategic negotiators use with great success.

Now that we have discussed the principles, strategies, and tactics of competitive negotiating, we will explore how strategic negotiators use cooperative negotiating techniques to get better deals. Ultimately, the best negotiators have an array of competitive and cooperative techniques that they use with the precision and effectiveness of a master craftsman. The owners of both small and large businesses need to be particularly effective at selecting the right tools to negotiate better deals: Too much cooperation can hurt business, and too little competition can reduce profits. The key to good driving is finding the best route to get to your destination. The most successful businesses make effective use of both competitive and cooperative negotiating techniques.

Key Points to Remember: Chapter 2

1. Strategic negotiators understand and use the dynamics of competitive negotiating to maximize value.

2. Competitive negotiating is predictable and, therefore, manageable.

3. Use the timing and size of concessions to manage the other negotiator's expectations.

4. Build your dance floor and dance.

5. Avoid short-circuiting the dance.

6. The end-point is usually at or near the mid-point between the first two reasonable offers.

7. Use the magnetic pull effect of the opening offer.

8. A reasonable opening offer should be worded firmly.

9. An extreme opening offer should be worded flexibly.

10. Use the powers of linkage and anchoring to close deals.

CHAPTER 3

Cooperative Negotiation

Creating Value by Bargaining for Mutual Gain

A student of ours once described the negotiator from hell. The student worked for a software developing firm. Each year, one of the firm's largest customers would send a brash young man to negotiate a new deal to purchase the firm's software products. The negotiations were the same each year. The customer's negotiator would come in, set up his laptop, and play a violent scene of conquest from one movie or another. At the end of this presentation, the negotiator would smile and say, "This is how we negotiate every deal." Point taken: He's a killer and he's going to get his way in the negotiation. No subtlety there.

How did the software firm's negotiators respond to dealing with this fellow? Physical illness, anxiety, disgust, and hatred are a few of the words they used to describe the experience. The customer had power in the relationship, however, so the aggressively competitive negotiator usually got a "great" deal, which to him meant the most product for the cheapest price. The software firm, however, refused to offer extras they might have offered another customer, including support services, all of which could have added value to the deal for the customer. The aggressively competitive negotiator left the table without securing everything that was available to him. Great negotiators do not do that.

This is an extreme example of competitive negotiating behavior, but it does illustrate a fundamental psychological reaction to competitiveness and the aggression it engenders. In our negotiation seminars, frequently we ask the students to perform this brief exercise.

> The class divides up into pairs and the students face each other, about two feet apart. One of the students in the pair is asked to form his or her fingers into a fist and extend the fist pointing upward about 10 inches from his or her face. Then, the other student is instructed that he or she has 60 seconds to get the other student to open his or her fist.

> Pandemonium ensues. Some students aggressively grab their partner's fist, trying to pry the fingers open, while the recipients of this onslaught vigorously resist. These interactions seem to follow a variation of Newton's Law; each application of force creates an equal and opposing force. The more aggressively force is applied to pry the fingers loose, the more aggressively the recipient resists. Fortunately, we stop the exercise well before anyone can be injured, but the point of the exercise becomes clear in the first several seconds: Aggressive competition breeds aggressive resistance.

Also imagine what aggressive competition does to business, personal, and organizational relationships. Some aggressively competitive people get what they want because those with whom they negotiate simply give in to get the experience over with or because they have no real bargaining power. But, these same aggressive negotiators kill many deals. Worse, overly competitive negotiation tactics can deprive negotiators of deals that better meet their needs, including lasting agreements that ensure unhindered perform- ance from the people whom they have beaten up. Aggressive competition can destroy the good will and trust necessary to implement the agreement. Aggressive competition undermines the cooperation and good will necessary to smoothly functioning employment, busi- ness, and personal relationships.

> **Negotiating Tip**
>
> Sometimes aggressive competition leaves unclaimed value on the table when you can get a better deal by negotiating cooperatively.

Thus, every effective, strategic negotiator gets the best deals by mastering the techniques of both competi- tive and cooperative negotiating. And cooperative nego- tiating requires a level of patience, sophistication, and people skills that naturally competitive people may find difficult to master. The good news is that naturally cooperative people will find this chapter a breath of fresh air after studying the strategies and tactics of competitive negotiating.

Integrative Bargaining:
Moving Beyond the Zero-Sum, Fixed-Pie Negotiation

Whether we like it or not, many of us default to the competitive, fixed pie negotiation because it is familiar. It is much easier to identify a fixed-pie of value—money, property—than it is to identify creative options that might yield elegant deals. Yet when we negotiate competitively, we may encourage escalation of conflict and distrust. Sometimes competitive negotiating does not create better deals.

The first step in cooperatively negotiating, or "integrative bargaining" as it is otherwise known, is to recognize when competitive negotiating will not get the job done. Typically, this happens when the parties are in an ongoing personal or business relationship, or negotiate frequently with each other. In other instances, the fixed pie the negotiators are trying to distribute through competitive negotiating cannot be divided that way, and it may be that they can reach agreement seeking creative ways of expanding that pie. Since competitive bargaining is hard on relationships and addresses only the fixed pie being distributed, cooperative negotiating techniques are among the most effective tools in the strategic negotiator's belt. Owners of successful businesses large and small rely on cooperative negotiating every day when competitive negotiating is a less effective tool to achieve their objectives.

> ## Definition
>
> Cooperative negotiating is expanding the pie by negotiating for mutual gain and creating value to be shared by both negotiators.

The second step in using a cooperative negotiating approach builds off of Axelrod's theory for avoiding exploitation by beginning cooperatively. Negotiating cooperatively requires that both negotiators accept a simple, fundamental, anti-competitive premise: They may create a mutually satisfying deal if they negotiate for shared gain. Some people call this "win/win" negotiation, but we think that is a little simplistic. The idea of cooperative negotiating is not to make the world a better place, although it would do that without question were it to be employed more frequently. No, cooperative negotiating is all about expanding the pie by creating value so that both negotiators can get what they need. Negotiating cooperatively involves far more patience, creativity, and innovation than competitive bargaining. The following are some simple guidelines to follow when implementing a cooperative negotiating strategy.

Step One of Cooperative Negotiating: It's the Language You Use

There have been many attempts to crystallize the techniques of cooperative negotiating into a simple set of guidelines. Perhaps one of the best-known efforts is that put forth by Fisher and Ury in their book *Getting to Yes* (Penguin Books, 1991). Since then, many negotiation professionals, communication theorists, and conflict resolution researchers have weighed in on the guidelines for negotiating cooperatively, that is, for shared gain. From this body of work, one can create a blueprint for negotiating cooperatively.

The fundamental strategy upon which cooperative negotiating is premised, and which dictates the first step, is that the language of the negotiation has to encourage cooperation, not competition. What does that mean as a practical matter? As Fisher and Ury put it best, you must "separate the people from the problem." They also refer to this step as being "soft on the people, hard on the issues." A cooperative negotiating approach dictates managing one's own words and perceptions to guide one's communication in a way that permits exploration of both negotiators' underlying needs and interests. By changing the language of the conversation to one of cooperation as opposed to one of competition, the strategically cooperative negotiator begins a process of exploring mutually satisfying options for reaching a deal. Better deals from better, more strategically managed communication. Or, as your mother may have told you, "You catch more flies with honey than you do with vinegar." That is the first step of cooperative negotiating in a nutshell.

Consider this fictional story of an employee who wants a raise. The employee—we'll call her Jill—has been working as an executive assistant for the same employer—a lawyer named Beth—for several years. Jill likes her job, but she has not received a raise in the last two years. She works very hard, and she believes she has contributed to Beth's and the law firm's success and profitability. She likes her boss, but she is intimidated by her. It is not that Beth is mean, but she is very busy, and she does not have a great deal of patience for long conversations. Still, Jill feels it is time to tell Beth she wants a raise. She decides what amount of pay increase she would accept, but she cannot decide on the right time to discuss it with Beth. Jill tries to begin the conversation on several occasions, but backs out at the last moment.

Over time, Jill becomes more frustrated, until one day she walks into Beth's office and asks to speak to her. Beth is very busy that day preparing for a meeting, and asks if the matter can wait. Jill, visibly shaking and upset, angrily says "Fine!," and storms out of the room. She stays sullen and angry for the next several days. Beth is left wondering whether Jill is losing it. In the next several weeks, Beth notices that Jill is less attentive, less communicative, and less efficient. Beth starts noticing that Jill is making more errors and seems distracted. As this continues, Beth becomes angry but remains quiet about her concerns, and the conflict escalates. In a short time, Jill announces that she is leaving for a job with another lawyer in town where she will make more money. Beth has lost a valuable employee and now she has to look for a suitable replacement, a time-consuming, difficult, and uncertain task. Jill enters a new work situation with a new boss and all the uncertainty and anxiety that implies. Both missed an important opportunity, they just do not realize it. Moreover, neither Jill nor Beth got what they wanted—a stable and mutually satisfying working relationship.

Negotiating Tip

We all feel that the people with whom we are in relationships should understand our needs without our having to express them. But the only way for people to learn about each other's needs is through communication.

This problem of communication between people in business and personal relationships is repeated millions of times each day. We all feel that the people with whom we are in relationships, personal or business, should know us well enough to understand our needs without our having to express them. But people are not terribly good at reading minds. The only way for people to learn about each other's needs and interests is to invite that information in some manner through communication. And that is the hard part, as we do not know how to do this well, either. Sharing our needs and interests risks vulnerability, particularly with people upon whom we may be dependent to some extent, or those with whom we have experienced conflict. We would rather remain silent and let our unmet needs simmer into resentment and anger.

In order to begin a negotiation about creating an agreement that meets the needs of both parties, the strategic negotiator understands that the language she chooses should nurture the relationship she has with the other negotiator, while at the same time clearly and firmly identifying the issue to be negotiated. The reason why Jill was afraid to have this conversation about what she needed was because she feared it would undermine her working relationship with her boss, Beth, and jeopardize her job. If Jill had behaved like a strategic negotiator, however, she could have begun the negotiation with language that respected her working relationship with Beth, while at the same time identifying her needs clearly and firmly.

For example, Jill did not need to wait so long to have the conversation with Beth. Waiting tends to increase anxiety, which in turn promotes anger and competition in the choice of language. Instead, Jill could have clearly defined her needs, then approached Beth when she was not overwhelmed. Jill might have told Beth, "At some point today or tomorrow, can I have about 15 minutes of your time to discuss something?" Beth would likely have listened intently to this, wondering what this important conversation would be about. Beth might even have said, "Of course. Tomorrow morning would be great. Can you give me an idea of what you would like to discuss with me?" Jill could have then said, "I would like to discuss my compensation with you." Beth might then have said, "Okay," or something like it, and the stage would have been set for a proper conversation in a cooperative setting.

> ### Step One of Cooperative Negotiating
>
> Be soft on the people, hard on the issue, and use language that encourages cooperation.

Notice that there is an element of competition in this negotiation before it even begins. Jill has an interest in maximizing her compensation, and Beth and the law firm have an interest in minimizing what Jill is paid, at least theoretically. But the working relationship between the employer and the employee, particularly the perceptions they each have of the value of that relationship, may greatly outweigh any inherent competition that exists in a salary increase negotiation. In other words, for both, the value of cooperation may be more important than the value of competition, thus favoring a cooperative negotiating approach.

Once the strategic objective of cooperation is fashioned, both negotiators can continue to use language that is "hard on the issue" but "soft on the people." The "issue" here is money. The "people" part of this negotiation is the value of the employment relationship to both parties. When Jill and Beth meet the next morning, the conversation might begin like this: "What do you have on your mind?" Beth might ask. Jill might respond, "Well, I really enjoy working for you, and I find my job rewarding and energizing on many levels. I feel I do my job exceptionally well. But the last time I had a raise was two years ago, and the pay I'm currently receiving is significantly less than what assistants of my experience and skill are receiving at other law firms in town. So I've given the matter a lot of thought, and I think a fair increase in my salary should be to $X."

In this example, Jill took care to reaffirm the value of the employment relationship and that her request for a salary increase (an opening offer) was anchored to an objectively reasonable standard of measure—the market. This use of language in the negotiation encourages a similar kind of response from the employer. Beth might respond, "Well, I've had a chance to think over your present compensation package, and I agree with you, it is time to review it. You are an excellent assistant, and I really value your work. As you know, however, the law firm has experienced lower revenue the last two years. I have not had a raise in that time, either. Things have recently improved, however, so I think that I can provide you with a salary increase that makes sense. Let me give the matter some more thought. Can I get back to you tomorrow on this?"

In the above example, both parties have managed the competitive and cooperative features of their negotiation through the strategic use of communication. They have taken care to reaffirm the value of their working relationship—they were "soft on the people"—while at the same time being clear and firm in their discussion of the money—"hard on the issue." They also have taken care to make their offers reasonable by anchoring them to an objective measure—for the employee, her market value; for the employer, the law firm's profitability. Similar negotiations happen every day in the business world in prospective employment, consumer sales, equipment and supplies purchases, and the list goes on. In these negotiations, the most successful negotiators use cooperative negotiating techniques to fashion elegant and sophisticated deals. Their success is not an accident of personality. They strategically manage communication and the balance between competition and cooperation to maximize value for both parties in their negotiations. Successful strategic negotiators master the language of cooperation to get better deals.

Step Two: Go Below the Line

How often do you know what the other negotiator is really thinking or feeling? Not often. We are not omniscient, and the best we can do to figure out what the other negotiator is thinking or feeling is to interpret his words and actions during the negotiation. As mentioned previously, strategic negotiators can learn a great deal from the other negotiator's moves. But even the best negotiators do not learn enough about the other negotiator's needs and interests from reading the tea leaves of the moves the parties make during the negotiation.

Every negotiator comes to the table with a set of underlying needs and interests he hopes to fulfill. When we talk about "needs" and "interests," we are really describing that rich tapestry of human concerns that shapes the positions negotiators take in negotiations (see Figure 3-1).

A negotiator's underlying interests have everything to do with why the negotiator takes certain positions in the negotiation. Yet the negotiator may be reluctant to share such sensitive, personal information with the other negotiator, particularly where rapport and trust have not been established. Additionally, many negotiators do not even understand their underlying

FIGURE 3-1. **Issues and Interests**

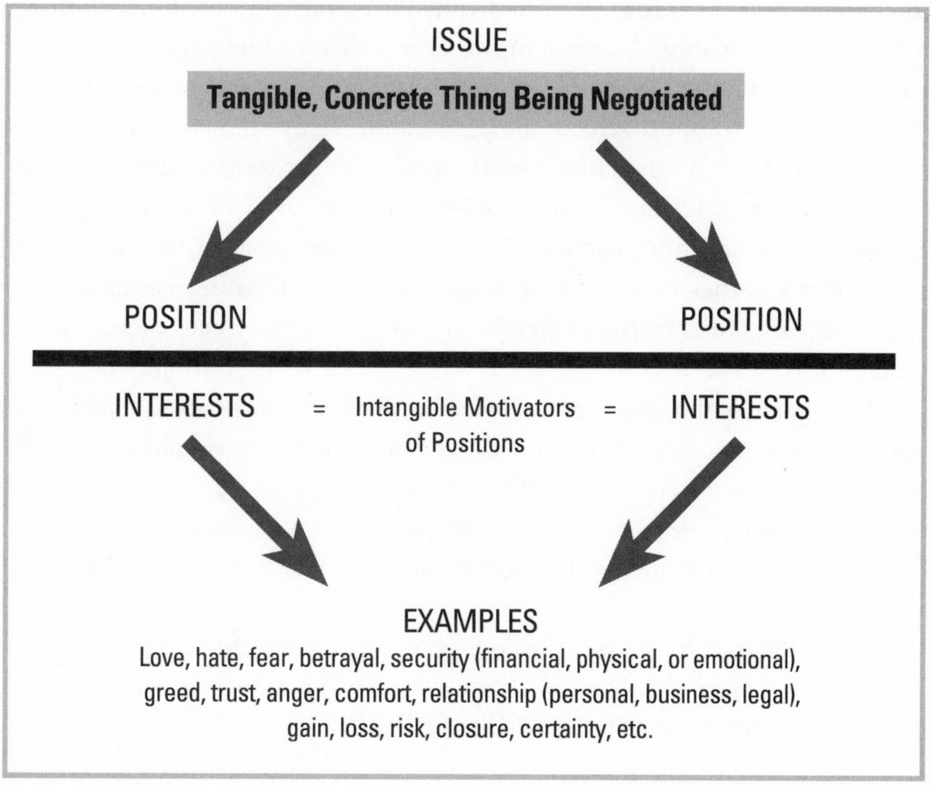

ISSUE

Tangible, Concrete Thing Being Negotiated

POSITION   POSITION

INTERESTS   =   Intangible Motivators   =   INTERESTS
                        of Positions

EXAMPLES

Love, hate, fear, betrayal, security (financial, physical, or emotional), greed, trust, anger, comfort, relationship (personal, business, legal), gain, loss, risk, closure, certainty, etc.

interests well enough to recognize them, let alone strategically manage the negotiation to achieve them. Many people negotiate reflexively and emotionally, not strategically. Their underlying interests will govern the positions they take in negotiations and these negotiators will not even realize it!

> **Negotiating Tip**
>
> The key to successfully using cooperative negotiating techniques is to understand the importance of underlying interests in creating the deal.

The key to successfully using cooperative negotiating techniques is to understand the importance of underlying interests in creating the deal. The strategic negotiator learns about the other negotiator's underlying interests for two reasons. First, if the two negotiators' interests are compatible and a deal can be reached by cooperative negotiating, then that information serves as the basis of such a negotiation. Second, if the negotiators' interests are incompatible, or if they need to divide a fixed pie of value, thus requiring competitive negotiating, learning the other negotiator's underlying interests is extremely valuable strategic information. Whether the strategic negotiator is using a cooperative approach, a competitive approach, or a mixture of the two, he or she can fashion offers that attempt to meet the other negotiator's underlying needs and interests. This increases the likelihood of reaching a deal because people are more likely to agree to proposals that satisfy their needs and interests sufficiently. This, in turn, makes for a lasting agreement. A durable agreement is worth its weight in gold. An illusory deal is more trouble than it is worth.

"Going below the line," that is, learning the other negotiator's underlying needs and interests, involves sophisticated communication techniques, including attentiveness, listening, and questioning. Often, we are much too impatient or too dependent on instant gratification in conversation to use these techniques to learn about another person's underlying interests. This brings to mind another story.

There was an elderly woman who lived in a 100-year-old farmhouse. We'll call her Mrs. Elderberry. She was a member of a well-respected farming family that had settled the town in which she lived. The character of the town, however, was rapidly changing. In the last 30 years, the town had evolved from a rural, agricultural community to a bustling suburban city. Tract homes, malls, and commercial office developments had sprouted around the woman's home. The city she now lived in was a far cry from the rural farming town in which she was born.

As a result of the changes occurring all around her, Mrs. Elderberry's home was on some of the most valuable real estate in the region. A series of commercial real estate developers began contacting Mrs. Elderberry to see if she was willing to sell her home and land. The developers who contacted her were masters of competitive negotiating, and they each offered Mrs. Elderberry increasingly generous sums of money to buy her property. These developers assumed that the most important thing to Mrs. Elderberry was the amount of money she would accept to part with her home. The developers assumed that a deal could be put together based upon money, and they negotiated about the tangible issues of money and land. They used the language with which they were the most familiar—competitive negotiating. We refer to this approach as staying "above the line."

Mrs. Elderberry politely but firmly declined each offer, leaving the developers to scratch their heads and wonder why they could not close the deal. "She must be one tough customer," many concluded, and they kept sweetening the pot, offering her more and more money. And Mrs. Elderberry kept saying "No." With each "above the line" approach, Mrs. Elderberry grew more steadfast. Eventually, she stopped taking calls from the developers. Mrs. Elderberry stayed in her home surrounded by commercial development she could not stand, lonely and isolated from her loved ones. The developers had offered twice the fair market value of the land, but they were no closer to acquiring it.

What was wrong with this picture? Theoretically, everyone has his or her price, right? At some point, the developers would offer Mrs. Elderberry a deal she could not refuse, right? Wrong. There was some important information the competitive, fixed-pie negotiators were never going to unearth. The developers were not such good negotiators after all. They had no clue about going below the line to learn about Mrs. Elderberry's underlying interests, and whether a deal could be fashioned to meet them. The result: To this day, that farmhouse sits surrounded by office buildings. Neither Mrs. Elderberry nor the developers got what they needed.

How could this negotiation have been handled differently? What if you were the developer's agent? You might have employed a cooperative negotiating approach by trying to establish some kind of rapport with Mrs. Elderberry. For example, you might have introduced yourself to Mrs. Elderberry in a polite, respectful way. She would likely have been distrustful, given the succession of clever developers who had tried to buy her off. She would know your game immediately, but you could be patient and transparent. "I am with ABC, and, yes, we do develop communities. But, I think you'll find we're a little different. We listen." Mrs. Elderberry might then have said, "Now, that would be a refreshing change!" You both might have laughed. And after spending some time sharing stories about family, and perhaps a meal, you could get down to business. "Tell me about this wonderful home. I'll bet it has a story to tell," you might have said. And, if you had established rapport, and some trust, you might be surprised at the information you would have received.

> **Negotiating Tip**
>
> The establishment of trust and rapport is an important—and often very productive—cooperative negotiating approach.

"Well, not too many people these days know that this house was built by my grandfather over 100 years ago. He was one of the four people who founded this town. It was a lot smaller then. And different, too. People knew each other. There were no cars, only horses. And so much farm land and so many trees. Beautiful trees. The air was clear, the neighbors were kind. It was a wonderful place in which to grow up." Mrs. Elderberry would probably have had a slightly sad, nostalgic look in her eyes.

"I was born in this house, as was my father. He died in this house. I raised five children in this house. I planted that garden in front, and the one in back, too. My grandfather planted every tree you see, and I like to think there's a part of my family history in every one." She would probably have seemed a little sadder. "This house, the garden, the trees . . . they are part of my family history, our legacy."

You might then have asked, "Do you see yourself in this house forever?" She might then have said, "That's a good question. I don't know. I'm 82 years old. My husband passed away five years ago, and my children have all moved away. I have ten grandchildren, but it's getting harder for them to come visit me here. And I'm finding it's harder for me to garden or take care of the house. It's so large and it has so many stairs. I have arthritis, and I just can't get around as well any more." Mrs. Elderberry would probably have appeared anxious as she said these things, like they had been weighing heavily on her mind.

What would you have learned in such a conversation? Mrs. Elderberry has plenty of underlying interests: nostalgia, family connection to the home, love of gardening and of trees, the rural character of the neighborhood and how it is changing, a desire to be closer to her family and grandchildren, her advancing age and health, her decreasing ability to care for the home and yard. While she resists the idea of selling the home, clearly she is trying to cope with the possibility of not being able to stay there any more. Is it possible she might be willing to sell it? Perhaps, but she is not yet prepared to make that decision. She needs more information.

> **Negotiating Tip**
>
> Gathering information and exploring alternatives are dynamic cooperative negotiation techniques that result in gain for both parties.

You then might have asked, "What if there was some way to get you closer to your grandchildren, in a more rural area with trees, in a smaller, more manageable home you loved, and we could do that in a way that honored your family's legacy and contributions to the community; would you be willing to explore ways we could do something like that?" Notice that this question asks Mrs. Elderberry whether she is willing to explore ways of meeting needs and interests she has already expressed. This is a polite invitation to a cooperative negotiation. Mrs. Elderberry then might have said that she was willing to enter into a cooperative negotiation where both parties mutually gain. Mrs. Elderberry might have

> **Definition**
>
> Going below the line means learning underlying interests through rapport, listening, and patient questioning.

said she was not ready to have such a negotiation. The point is that the developers who kept offering Mrs. Elderberry money did not even get this far. They could not open the door to putting together a deal. Proper use of a cooperative negotiating approach, particularly establishing rapport, listening, and asking questions designed to elicit information about Mrs. Elderberry's underlying needs and interests, is the only way a deal would have any chance of coming together in this instance.

If Mrs. Elderberry expressed interest in discussing the sale of her property, in what kinds of ways could the woman's underlying interests be met? The home could be moved to a new location at the developer's expense; the home could be removed and an office building could be named in her family's honor; a museum dedicated to the family's and the community's history could be located in the new office building; a home with garden, trees, and a nice neighborhood could be found closer to her grandchildren and necessary amenities; the new home could be easier for her to navigate and maintain. There are many possible options for meeting her needs. Blindly offering her money and trusting that at some point she will say "yes" prevented the first developers from learning about Mrs. Elderberry's underlying interests, which were the keys to creating a deal. Rapport, listening, and patient questioning is the only way this information can ever be revealed to the negotiator's benefit.

A word of caution is in order. It would be a perfect world if we could always feel comfortable enough to risk vulnerability and exploitation by divulging our underlying interests. But that is not the real world. When using a cooperative negotiating approach, you must realize that strategic negotiators should not share their underlying interests unless the exchange of information is reciprocal. Otherwise, a cooperative negotiator could be exploited by a competitive negotiator who is just pretending to be cooperative. A strategic negotiator can be very effective at maximizing value by using a cooperative approach to competitive negotiating, so one should always be strategic in revealing one's underlying needs and interests. Cooperative negotiating produces mutual gain when both negotiators share information concerning their underlying interests and demonstrate a willingness to fashion an agreement that is mutually satisfying. Like all negotiating behavior, each negotiator should share information when it is strategically advantageous to do so.

Step Three: Creating Options with the Potential for Mutual Gain

Once the strategic negotiator establishes an element of rapport and trust by being "soft on the people, hard on the issue," (in other words, by learning the other negotiator's underlying interests and by sharing her own underlying needs and interests), the next step is to create options that might meet both parties' interests. This is a delicate step in the negotiation process because both negotiators must feel comfortable enough to share their ideas—to brainstorm, if you will. In order to do this effectively, there are some guidelines:

- *No Criticism.* First, the negotiators must commit to identifying all potential options for mutually meeting their interests. In order to do so, the negotiators also must agree to refrain from evaluating or criticizing the options until they have concluded the identification process. Nothing dampens brainstorming more than criticism of an idea at the beginning of the process. The option-generation stage is the ultimate "what if" moment. All potential ideas should be identified, even ones that are far-out or may have little chance of working. The idea here is to cast a wide net. In order to do this effectively, all participants in brainstorming must feel comfortable sharing their ideas.

- *No Commitment.* Second, the negotiators must agree that by creating options with the potential for mutual gain, they are not expressing or suggesting any commitment to the ideas they discuss. This protects the negotiators against their statements being perceived as offers. To avoid this problem, all negotiators must agree that they will not use any statements as offers or proposals.

- *Develop the Options.* Third, after the negotiators have come up with a list of potential options, they must develop them. This is the "what does it look like?" moment. Each option on the list should be fleshed out. Once that has been accomplished, it will become apparent which options are more workable than others. The options can be ranked later from more workable to less workable.

- *Evaluate the Options.* Fourth, evaluate the list of possible options to see which ones have some chance of being mutually acceptable. This is the "will it work?" moment. At this point, each negotiator must individually evaluate the options to see which ones best meet his or her needs. It is at this stage of the creative process of cooperative negotiating that the parties will negotiate over the list of options. Some give and take will need to take place in order for a common set of options to be agreed upon.

- *No Quitting.* Finally, from the outset and throughout the process of brainstorming, the participants must agree that they will not quit; they will continue with the process of creating, developing, and evaluating options with the potential for mutual gain until they have exhausted all potential solutions or reached agreement. This ensures that a breakthrough moment is not lost because the parties failed to continue with the brainstorming process. Sometimes the most elegant solutions emerge from brainstorming after several cycles of option creation, development, and evaluation have occurred.

If there is an option or options upon which both negotiators agree, a deal has been reached. If not, the negotiators may need to go back to the option generation process to either develop existing options or create new ones. This can sometimes be frustrating. At this point, the parties may need to take a break and negotiate later after they have had a chance to reflect on the possible options for mutual agreement. Frequently, this results in a breakthrough later.

The process of creating options for mutual gain takes discipline, patience, and the ability to think outside the box. In particular, creating options requires each negotiator to look at the issues from each other's perspectives. This is a critical tool of cooperative negotiating. The most successful negotiators understand that the best way to create options for mutual gain is to look at the problem from the point of view of the other negotiator's underlying interests. This skill permits us to offer options that meet our own needs while at the same time being attractive to the other negotiator.

Cooperative Negotiating in Action: Working Together to Solve the Problem

Cooperative negotiating can be used in a variety of settings, as the previous discussion illustrates. Here are two more examples of the power of cooperative negotiating to shape elegant solutions and durable agreements.

> **Brainstorming**
>
> 1. Identify all potential options (withhold criticism)—"What If?"
> 2. Develop options with potential for mutual gain—"What's it look like?"
> 3. Evaluate potential options—"Will It Work?"
> 4. Select options or begin again.

A Drunk-Driving, Wrongful-Death Lawsuit

Two teenagers were riding their bicycles through a state park when a park maintenance truck struck and killed them both. The driver, a state employee, was intoxicated. The parents of the two victims filed a lawsuit against the state for negligent supervision of this employee, who had a history of alcohol abuse on the job. Both sides were represented by attorneys. After years of litigation, and about two months before trial, the two sides decided to hold a settlement negotiation.

The negotiation was attended by the state representatives, their attorneys, the parents of the two children, and their attorneys. After hours of competitive negotiating, they reached an impasse. The state offered $800,000 to settle the lawsuit, and the parents demanded $1.2 million. For its part, the state had done extensive research about jury verdicts in wrongful death cases, and its offer reflected approximately 95 percent of its estimate of what the jury verdict likely would be, a very fair proposal. The parents did not see it that way: Their children had died. How dare the state try to put a price tag on their lives that was less than one million dollars?

The parties decided that they could not reach agreement. As the lawyers began packing their briefcases, the mother of the two victims shook her head and said, "You just don't get it." One of the state's lawyers stopped what he was doing and, looking at the mother, he asked, "What don't we get?" The mother was silent. The lawyer motioned for the state's representatives to sit back down, and he asked again in a patient, kind way, "Please tell me. I want to know. What don't we get?" The mother began to cry, and she said, "Our children deserve to be remembered."

> **Negotiating Tip**
>
> To uncover underlying interests, listen carefully to what is said, and, perhaps most importantly, to what is *not* being said.

Having asked that simple question, the state's lawyers asked the parents and their attorneys to stay and talk a bit longer. During the brainstorming session that followed, the state and the parents, with the assistance of their lawyers, explored ways that the parties might work together so that the children might be remembered. The parents had taken the position that the only fit way of remembering them would be for the amount of money to be at least one million dollars. Otherwise, their lives would not be sufficiently valued, and the city would not be held accountable. The state could not pay more than the reasonable settlement value of the case. So long as they continued with competitive negotiating, the money gap could not be closed.

But now the discussion moved in a direction focusing on underlying interests. And in that environment, both sides created options to meet their underlying interests. What they produced was something that could never have happened in court: The family agreed to accept a money settlement of $850,000, and the state agreed to erect a monument in the park and a bike path in the memory of the children. A full settlement was reached with the state meeting its interests in keeping the monetary settlement within a responsible range and avoiding a costly trial. The parents' core interest in honoring the memory of their children was fully satisfied in a way that competitive negotiating could never accomplish. More importantly, the agreement included a tangible monument to the memory of their children, something that a judge would have no power to order in the judgment had the case proceeded to trial. The state was able to meet that underlying interest of the parents for less money than the $400,000 that separated the parties at the end of competitive negotiating.

Here, a sophisticated, strategic negotiator recognized the expression of an underlying interest and shifted from competitive to cooperative negotiating accordingly. He used questioning and listening techniques to uncover the parents' hidden interests. He then created an environment in which the parties could brainstorm options for mutually meeting their underlying interests. This is what the best negotiators do. Underlying interests have a habit of expressing themselves during competitive negotiations because they are not being met. The key is recognizing them and finding a way to meet them. That is how better deals are made.

A Dispute Between a Bank and Its Software Provider

A large bank entered into a ten-year contract with a software firm to provide and maintain the bank's main transactional software program. The software firm had the best product on the market. The contract called for payment to the software firm of $1 million per year for the full ten years. This was a big contract for both parties, but particularly for the software firm. No one would jeopardize this kind of business relationship, right?

At the end of the first year of the contract, the software firm submitted an invoice to the bank that included $30,000 in expenses associated with the software firm's design engineers receiving training from the top expert in the world. The majority of these expenses were for travel to the expert's yacht in the Caribbean. The bank was incensed that it was being asked to pay for an obviously frivolous expense. It refused to pay the invoice. The software firm insisted that the expert was the only person in the world who provides this essential training, and that he insisted on doing the training on his yacht in the Caribbean. The bank did not buy that explanation. The software firm filed a lawsuit against the bank to recover the $30,000. All of a sudden, a lucrative $10 million business relationship was in mortal peril.

The parties hired aggressive lawyers who litigated this case for months. As the lawsuit began to escalate, a law student clerking at one of the big law firms involved asked the senior partner handling the case for one of the parties why no one had tried mediation as a way of negotiating a resolution. Mediation is a process in which a neutral third party, the mediator, assists the parties in attempting to negotiate an agreement. The partner had not given it much thought. He discussed the idea with his client who agreed to try to negotiate a resolution. Surprisingly, both parties agreed to hire a mediator to help them negotiate a resolution to the litigation.

> **Negotiating Tip**
>
> Cooperative negotiating works best when the negotiators try to see the negotiation from each other's point of view.

The negotiations at the mediation were difficult. The initiation of legal proceedings escalated the conflict, so the parties were angry and distrustful of each other. The mediator, however, understood that competitive bargaining in this environment was not likely to be successful. The parties had been competitively negotiating over the $30,000 invoice, which simply escalated the conflict. Instead, the mediator spent time privately with each side learning about their underlying interests. Eventually, the mediator brought the two CEO's together, and they were able to begin a cooperative negotiating discussion in which they shared their underlying interests.

The bank CEO learned that the expert in the Caribbean was, indeed, the only person who could provide training concerning the bank's financial software system. The software firm was not trying to pull the wool over the bank's eyes. The training enabled the software firm's design and technical staff to keep up to date with the rapid changes in this particular software operating system. The software firm did not want to be working with ten-year-old technology at the end of the contract. The bank's CEO agreed that updating the technology at regular intervals was beneficial to the bank. The software firm prided itself in staying current with technological innovation, and it perceived that the training session in question was essential to properly serving its clients, including the bank.

The software firm's CEO learned that the bank had a strong institutional interest in not paying for "training" expenses. This had resulted in a firm policy that employees would not be reimbursed for such expenses. This had been a particularly fertile area of corporate malfeasance in recent years, with CEOs and managers abusing their expense accounts to take vacations. Preventing these abuses and accounting to its shareholders was a crucial underlying interest of the bank. Word of the Caribbean training trip had become known to the bank's employees, so the bank had a heightened concern about sending a message that expenses like this would not be reimbursed under any circumstances.

Once the parties shared their underlying interests, they were amenable to brainstorming options with the potential for mutual gain. Notice that the two CEOs were able to establish rapport and the first steps of trust in this discussion. They were respectful toward each other and indicated an agreement in principle to find a way of meeting the two companies' underlying interests. The negotiators having established the legitimacy of their respective underlying interests, effective brainstorming ensued. After listing many options for trying to solve the dispute, the bank CEO asked an important question of the software firm CEO: "You said that this training offered by this fellow in the Caribbean is the only training of its kind in the world, right?" The software firm CEO confirmed this. The bank CEO then asked, "And most major financial institutions utilize this software operating platform, right?" The software firm CEO agreed.

Then, the important "what if" moment arrived. The bank CEO then said, "This looks like a business opportunity to me. What if we, the bank and your firm, were to form a joint venture to provide this training on an exclusive basis to financial institutions utilizing this software platform worldwide? We would be the only providers, right?" A light bulb went off in the software firm CEO's mind. "Correct," he said. The bank CEO then asked, "How much money would it take to start up this firm, including marketing for the first year?" The software firm CEO smiled. "I think $30,000 would be a fair contribution from the bank toward the start-up costs."

> **Negotiating Tip**
>
> When both negotiators agree that they are trying to find a mutually acceptable way to solve a common problem, brainstorming can produce elegant solutions.

An agreement was reached that day in which the bank and the software firm formed a company to provide training to all financial institutions concerning this software operating system. Any costs incurred to train the employees of the software firm and the bank concerning operation of the software system would be paid for by the new company. These costs would be recouped by the revenue the new company generated from providing training to other financial institutions concerning the software operating system. The bank would pay $30,000 as its initial investment in the start-up of that company. That company proved immensely profitable and survives to this day. The bank has long since evaporated in the seemingly endless evolution of financial institutions through mergers and competition.

> **Definition**
>
> Cooperative negotiating means moving from opposite sides of the table to the same side of the table.

Cooperative negotiating was introduced to this problem well after it should have been employed. Sometimes, however, wisdom takes time to reveal itself. The two companies saw an opportunity that only could have emerged with the process of cooperative negotiating. Competitive negotiating kept that door shut. When cooperative negotiating opens that door, however, truly elegant solutions can emerge.

As we conclude our discussion about the techniques of cooperative negotiating, we would like you to perform an illuminating exercise. In Figure 3-2, you see there are nine dots. Your task is to connect the nine dots in four straight lines. Once your pen touches the paper, however, it must stay in continuous contact with the paper until you have completed the task (no lifting the pen). The most common solution to the task is seen in Figure 3-3.

If you did not figure out a way to connect the nine dots, the odds are very good that you did not believe you could draw any lines outside the rectangle in which the dots were arrayed. Even though the instructions did not require you to keep your lines within that box, your mind created the box, and your creativity was restricted accordingly. What is the significance of this exercise? Creativity requires "thinking outside the box." The "box" is the rigid or

FIGURE 3-2. **The Nine Dot Exercise**

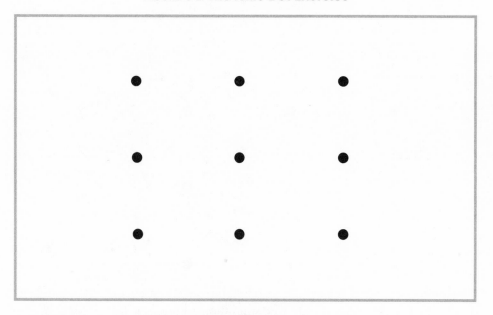

inflexible concept we may form about how to solve a problem. Using the power of cooperative negotiating means looking beyond the "box" to embrace potential solutions that best meet the parties' underlying needs and interests, even those that seem far-out or that have been previously rejected. Effective strategic negotiators create elegant deals by thinking outside the box. When we are not limited by thinking of these nine dots as a box, we are liberated to connect them by drawing the lines well outside the box, as Figure 3-3 reveals.

Your negotiator's tool belt should contain all the techniques of competitive and cooperative negotiating. Your task is to make strategic decisions about which of those tools to use in which situations. That is the challenge, and the fun, of negotiating. There is one group of people who have used the power of cooperative negotiating to create some of the most innovative business agreements in modern history: entrepreneurs. No business owner should be without the important tool of cooperative negotiating in her belt.

FIGURE 3-3. **Thinking Outside the Box**

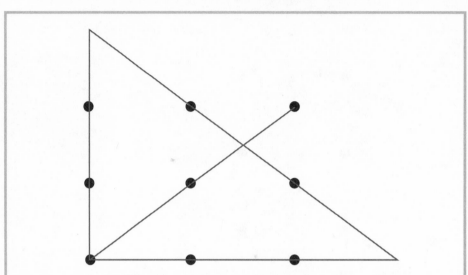

Key Points to Remember: Chapter 3

1. Some deals cannot be closed by using competitive negotiating.

2. Cooperative negotiating = expanding the pie by creating value.

3. Step One: Be soft on the people, hard on the issue.

4. Step Two: Go below the line to learn underlying interests.

5. Going below the line = Rapport, listening, and patient questioning.

6. Step Three = Create options with potential for mutual gain by brainstorming.

7. Cooperative negotiating = Working together to solve a problem.

8. Creativity and innovation require thinking outside the box.

9. Cooperative negotiating means that the negotiators try in good faith to meet each other's needs.

10. If there is no agreement, begin again with Step One.

CHAPTER 4

Dealing with Difficult Negotiation Situations

As the saying goes, "It takes all kinds." We all interact with people who are different from us every day. Frequently, our interactions are surprisingly positive. Often, our experiences are benign or indifferent. Other times, we encounter people we hope to never see again. This range of experience is repeated and magnified in our negotiations. Because negotiating involves people communicating in an attempt to get what they perceive they want or need, the opportunities for negative interactions and difficult moments increase exponentially. Sometimes people are so afraid of these negative moments happening, that they try to avoid negotiating at all costs or they give in quickly so they can end the experience as soon as possible. Neither approach is a strategic way of dealing with the difficult situations that arise in negotiations.

Often, we assume that the negative experience we are having with the other negotiator is his or her fault. We might think the other negotiator is "stupid," or "difficult," or "frustrating," or "lying." But such conclusions are typically speculative and inaccurate. Instead, more commonly, these feelings reflect our own frustration with not getting what we want or need in the negotiation. It is easier for us to conclude the problem lies with the other negotiator than it is for us to blame ourselves. As the preceding chapters demonstrate, however, whether the communication process that is a negotiation succeeds or fails depends upon our own strategic management of it. We can control much of the difficulty we encounter in negotiations through thoughtful self-management. And sometimes, the problem is not with the other negotiator—it is in our own behavior.

Still, many times we must respond to the other negotiator's behaviors that might upset or unnerve us. These behaviors may be "tactics" intentionally employed by the other negotiator to take us out of our negotiating game. Other times, the other negotiator's words and actions may be unintentional and simply a product of his or her personality and communication style. Whether the other negotiator is employing a tactic or unintentionally behaving in a way that makes communication with him or her difficult, there are several ways that strategic negotiators can manage these situations to reach better deals.

Negative Behaviors and Tactics

What kinds of tactics and behaviors can take us out of our game? The following is a partial list we have culled together from years of asking this question to our students and drawing upon our own experiences:

- Yelling
- Physical intimidation
- Bullying
- Ultimatums

- Verbal abuse
- Ignoring
- Racist or sexist comments
- Tardiness
- Sarcasm
- Crying
- Last bite of the apple

- Silence
- Insults
- Unresponsiveness
- Lying
- Interrupting
- Good cop/Bad cop
- Lack of authority

We all can point to instances in which we have experienced these tactics and behaviors. But how do they make us feel? Angry, hurt, sick to our stomachs, anxious, trembling, confused, accommodating, resistive, worried. That is the point, is it not? If any of the above behaviors is being strategically employed as a negotiating tactic, then any of these reactions indicates that the tactic has been successful. If the other negotiator is behaving in any of these ways unintentionally, that is, not strategically, the effect is still the same—your negotiating game is being negatively affected. Typically, the things you say and do in this environment are not strategic at all, they are reactive. You do not get better deals when this occurs.

When we react to tactics or negative behaviors, the experience is primal and immediate. The brain does not engage, and words and actions just seem to come out of us automatically in response to the tactic or behavior. One of our colleagues related to us a story of a lawyer who had one of these moments during a settlement negotiation. The lawyer, who we will call Joe, is bald. He walked into the negotiating room, which was already occupied by a heavy-set attorney and his assistant. Joe politely said "Hello," and the other lawyer, without missing a beat, said, "Hello. It looks like they sent 'Baldy' to negotiate for your side today." To which Joe responded, without missing a beat, "Yep. And it looks like they sent 'Fatso' to negotiate for your side." That negotiation got off to a terrible start. No deal was reached that day.

If Joe's objective was to reach an agreement, did he manage the moment well? It depends. Maybe throwing the insult back was Joe's way of letting the other negotiator know that the tactic of insulting him about his physical appearance was not going to work. If Joe strategically managed his response

Negotiating Tip

The key to self-management is to identify the tactic or negative behavior, and evaluate the strategic response.

to neutralize the tactic, great. But Joe would be the first to admit that he had not engaged his strategic thinking at all. He reacted in anger with predictable results. And that is not what strategic negotiators do.

Thus, the key to dealing with tactics and negative behaviors in a negotiation is the same as that for successful strategic management generally: manage or be managed. The strategic negotiator must identify the tactic or negative behavior and evaluate his or her response to it. That step alone encourages the negotiator to stop, look, and listen. This, in turn, helps the strategic negotiator break the circuit between the stimulus and the response. Once that connection of action and reaction is broken, the negotiator can then evaluate what the strategic response should be.

Strategic Responses to Negative Behaviors and Tactics

The first step in managing your response to a tactic or negative behavior is to take a deep breath and think for a moment what the strategic response should be. Understanding that you *can* control the seemingly uncontrollable primal emotions you feel is the key to anger management. Some people use a visualization technique when a situation causes anger or fear to rear its ugly head. They may picture it beginning to rain and see themselves getting an umbrella, or some similar imagery. Others think of audible cues, such as a bell going off. Breaking the connection between stimulus and response is the key to self management, and how you do it is a question of what works for you.

If you succeed in halting the automatic response that wells up inside you in reaction to a tactic or negative behavior during a negotiation, you have several strategic choices available to you about what to do next.

Ignore the Tactic/Behavior

Frequently, the most effective strategic approach is to ignore the tactic or behavior. This tends to rob the tactic or behavior of its power, thus reducing its effectiveness. If our friend Joe had tried this approach, he might have paused, smiled, and said, "Good morning, I'm Joe. And you are . . . .?" The other negotiator might get the point: Joe is a pro and he will not be easily intimidated. The tactic of insulting Joe did not work, so perhaps the other negotiator will act more cooperatively.

The negative possibility with this approach is that the other negotiator may perceive that the tactic or behavior did not get through to you, so he or she ups the ante with a more extreme tactic or behavior. For example, if Joe responded by smiling and ignoring the tactic, the other negotiator might have tried something more extreme, such as "Apparently, you do not hear very well, either." Ignoring a tactic or behavior runs the risk of communicating weakness to the other negotiator and can invite him or her to attempt to exploit you. Sometimes, the most effective thing to do is to deal with the tactic or behavior directly.

Tactic Back

Our friend Joe used this approach: When the other negotiator used an insult, Joe insulted the fellow right back. Of course, this response is most frequently employed by people reactively and angrily rather than strategically. Still, remember Axelrod's theory of avoiding exploitation—you should begin a negotiation cooperatively, but be prepared to respond to competition with competition. The same principle applies with tactics; sometimes the most effective response to a tactic is a strategically reciprocal tactic.

For example, suppose someone uses the tactic of derogatory and sarcastic humor to put you down in a group of negotiators. You might strategically respond, first with silence and a smile, and then with a reciprocal derogatory and sarcastic remark. This would communicate that the tactic did not work and that you can play that game, too. Women find that this is frequently a good tactical response to put-down humor directed to them by men in negotiations.

The problem with responding to a tactic with a tactic is two-fold. First, the negotiation may turn into an antagonistic, positional, and competitive contest that defeats any kind of deal, but especially one that could be created through cooperative negotiating. Second, you might mistake an unintentional negative behavior for an intentional tactic. By doing so, you will have attributed a negative intention to something that may simply be an honest expression of an underlying interest. Rather than strategically using this as information to try to engage in cooperative negotiating, you will have simply escalated conflict by responding with a negative behavior.

For example, suppose Bill and Julie are negotiating the purchase of equipment. Julie is the seller's representative and Bill is the buyer's representative. Julie makes a sales presentation to Bill, and his staff, which consists of three other men. As Julie begins her video presentation, she starts by asking the group of men, "Have you had a chance to review my proposal?" Bill appears irritated by the question, and he answers, "Yes, Julie. We customarily read the proposals prior to these meetings." His staff snickers. Julie thinks to herself, "Great, another sexist jerk who's trying to make my life difficult." Julie may label the man's behavior as a tactic to take her out of her game. Her negative reaction will influence the negotiation in a bad way.

What Julie did not know is that Bill was in the midst of a power struggle with one of his senior staff, who was present in the room. Bill was under pressure to bring costs down, and he felt under the microscope during Julie's presentation. He was irritated by Julie's suggestion that he might not have come to the meeting prepared. He prides himself on being prepared, and expects all with whom he deals to have a similar approach. Labeling Bill's behavior as a negative tactic, rather than the expression of an underlying interest in handling this purchase professionally and in a way that cannot be criticized by a competitor, would be a grave mistake in this negotiation. Julie might even have used the tactic of silence to act on her feelings of anger at Bill, a move that would have posed problems in negotiating a deal.

Since responding to a tactic or negative behavior with a tactic or negative behavior can escalate competition and conflict, and is more likely to be a non-strategic response, this approach should be used with great caution and only sparingly.

Confront the Tactic or Behavior, and Negotiate the Process

One of the most effective means of strategically managing a tactic or negative behavior during a negotiation is to identify it, confront it, and negotiate what the process of your negotiation will be.

For example, a lawyer we know encountered a tactic employed by opposing counsel during preparation of a case arising from a business dispute. At the beginning of the case, our colleague grew perturbed because the other lawyer never returned her phone calls. Before calling the lawyer again, our colleague identified the tactic employed—ignoring our colleague and making her initiate contact with the other lawyer—and fashioned a strategic response. She called the lawyer's office again, this time reaching him. As their conversation began, our colleague said, "You know, I've noticed that you have not returned several phone calls that I've made. We are going to be communicating by phone and mail a lot in this case, and we can do that a number of different ways. If you want, I can decide not to get back to you when you call. But I don't think that will be very efficient or useful. Perhaps we can reach an agreement that we will return each other's calls within 48 hours. Does that work for you?" After that, the other lawyer returned our colleague's calls within the designated 48-hour period, and the two lawyers were able to work effectively with each other.

Confronting the tactic and negotiating process is extraordinarily effective. It invites the other negotiator to manage his or her own behavior as a strategic means of getting what he or she needs in the negotiation. It is also an effective way of separating the people from the problem, a key step in cooperative negotiating. Confronting the tactic and negotiating the process of the negotiation is also an assertion of control or power by one negotiator that invites the other negotiator to assert a reciprocal level of positive control over the negotiation. This approach also separates the emotions from the moment and places the focus of communication on the creation of a process that can produce a deal. Reacting to a negative

> **Negotiating Tip**
>
> Being the driver of the negotiation means managing your response to negative behaviors and intentional tactics, not letting your response manage you.

behavior or tactic without confronting it and trying to change the language of the negotiation usually results in failure for both negotiators.

Therefore, the strategic negotiator has several ways of effectively addressing intentional tactics or negative behaviors. You should pick the approach that has the greatest probability of fostering a productive negotiation.

Dealing with Strong Emotions

Sometimes during a negotiation, we can confuse the expression of strong emotions with tactics or negative behaviors. That is because we all have varying degrees of comfort or discomfort with the expression of emotions. Those of us who are uncomfortable with emotional situations have predictable ways we respond when those with whom we are negotiating become angry or upset; we might stop the negotiation, respond defensively, grow silent, or do anything to make the discomfort go away. Any of these reactions is likely to produce no deal or a worse deal for a simple reason: Sometimes a negotiator's expression of strong emotions provides useful information about his or her underlying interests, and suppressing or ignoring those interests may undermine the negotiation. People want to have their underlying needs and interests met in the negotiation; they will not participate in a negotiation that they perceive does not address those needs and interests.

The first step to dealing with strong emotions during a negotiation is to evaluate whether the emotional outburst is a tactic, a negative behavior, or simply an expression of emotion. This process of evaluation sets the stage for a strategic response. It also calms the mind and impedes an emotionally reactive response. There are several possible strategies for dealing with strong emotions during a negotiation.

Ignore Them

You can strategically decide to ignore the expression of strong emotions. This occasionally might be advisable, such as when the expression of strong emotions is normal for an individual or in a given culture. Strong emotional

expression may simply be an accepted part of the dialogue and there is no need to react to or manage it.

In other instances, however, ignoring a person's
strongly emotional statement during a negotiation is inappropriate and counterproductive. Like all communication
in the negotiation process, strong emotional expressions
carry information that the strategic negotiator must evaluate. When people communicate their emotions, they are
vulnerable and they are expressing some sort of a need.

> **Negotiating Tip**
>
> A negotiator's expression of strong emotions might be an important clue to his or her underlying interests.

The strategic negotiator understands this and asks, "What is this person telling
me and how is it useful in putting together a deal?" Perhaps the expression of
emotion is communicating that the negotiation is not addressing an underlying
interest. The strategic negotiator will see this and begin the process of discov-
ering the underlying interests of the other negotiator in an attempt to negotiate
cooperatively for shared gain. A perfect example of this occurred in the wrongful death/personal injury lawsuit negotiation referred to in the last chapter.

Here is another (fictional) example. The owner of a pet grooming shop,
who we will call Sandra, has a regular customer we will call Frank. One day,
Frank brings his long-haired dog into Sandra's shop for a bath and grooming.
Sandra has advised Frank on many prior occasions to make sure that the dog
is brushed regularly to get out mats. Frank is somewhat disorganized and he
never gets around to doing so. On this particular day, when Sandra sees the
dog's snarled fur, she gets angry and says, "Frank, I've told you before, you
need to brush these mats out. This is terrible." Frank is offended, thinks
Sandra has been rude, and quietly decides this is the last time he will go to
Sandra's shop. This is a shame, as Sandra is the only pet grooming business in
his town and she does an excellent job at a reasonable price. If Frank responds
angrily and with the tactics of silence and avoidance, he will lose a valuable and
convenient service and Sandra will lose a regular customer. Neither negotiator will get what he or she wants.

Since continuing the business relationship is valuable to Frank, he might
have considered responding by asking for more information. "I know you've

said that before, Sandra, but I work long hours and I have very little time to brush Cody. Why is my brushing him regularly so important to you?" Sandra might have responded, "Well, when the fur gets as matted as Cody's is now, I

can not brush it out. I must cut the clumps with an electric razor, which does not look good, risks cutting Cody's skin, and is painful to him." Cody's appearance and comfort are important to Frank, so his temptation to respond by anger and silence would not have been either strategic or beneficial. Quelling those reactions and seeking further information was the right thing to do.

Additionally, sometimes the most culturally appropriate response to an expression of extreme emotion, such as crying over the loss of a loved one, is to express empathy and to say something supportive or reassuring. Impassively ignoring such an emotional expression might be seen as socially or culturally inappropriate and unkind. This, in turn, can impede the rapport and communication essential to effectively negotiating a deal. Therefore, ignoring a strong expression of emotion is advisable only in rare instances and only after evaluating its strategic and situational appropriateness.

Discourage Them

Another strategic choice is to discourage the expression of strong emotions. The moment the other negotiator begins to cry, or yells in anger, you might be tempted to tell him or her to stop. "That is not what we're talking about," you might say in an attempt to focus on what you think is important. The other person grows even more agitated, and the negotiation accomplishes nothing. This pattern of interaction is repeated millions of times per day. Sometimes, discouraging the expression of emotions does more harm than good. And, again, think about what information the emotional statement might contain. Might the other negotiator be revealing an underlying interest that the strategic negotiator might try to address in the process of using a cooperative negotiating approach? Might not empathy and reassurance address the other negotiator's emotions in a strategic way that de-escalates tensions and sets the stage for effective negotiating?

There are, however, times when discouraging certain types of emotional comments might be a good strategic choice. For example, a colleague of ours tells the story of a mediation she conducted between a husband and wife who were divorcing. At the point when the two began to discuss dividing the property, the wife began to cry, and the mediator handed her a tissue. As the wife was crying, the husband, who looked unmoved and somewhat annoyed, said to the mediator, "She does this every time we are about to talk about money. It's her way of getting sympathy. It's not going to work on me this time." With that, the wife stopped crying, muttered, "Oh, crap," and settled down to a very business-like discussion. Sometimes emotional expressions are manipulative or intended as a tactic, and identifying them as such and confronting them is a sound strategic approach.

Other times, emotional expressions are strongly negative, abusive, and counterproductive. They may also signal the negotiator's inability to manage his or her emotions and anger. Sometimes strong emotional outbursts are an intuitive or intentional way negotiators gain power in the negotiation. In those situations, emotional outbursts can be discouraged by negotiating process, that is, by setting certain ground rules for the negotiation. If the other negotiator cannot conform to them, then the negotiation can be terminated. This might be the only way of continuing the negotiation or avoiding power imbalance. It takes two to tango; both negotiators need to feel that the negotiation is working for them, otherwise the negotiation will fail.

Encourage and Manage Them

Another strategic approach may be to encourage the expression of emotions as a means of permitting venting and to uncover underlying interests. When people act emotionally, they can become very vulnerable. Validating their emotions can build the rapport and trust essential to cooperative negotiating. Encouraging emotional expressions can also assist discussion of underlying interests, which is an indispensable step in cooperative negotiating. Many

Negotiating Tip

If emotional expressions are encouraged, manage them with clear behavioral guidelines to which both negotiators agree (e.g., not interrupting, use of respectful language, equal opportunity to speak).

good things can come from the initial discomfort of emotional expressions. It is just a question of how the strategic negotiator manages the often difficult moments in a negotiation when people become emotional.

Of course, if one elects to encourage emotional expressions, one should be prepared to actively manage the resulting negotiating process or things could get out of hand. Setting behavioral guidelines, such as not interrupting and use of respectful language, can be helpful in managing emotional moments. Use of empathy and validation can also be very helpful. For example, if the other negotiator gets very emotional in discussing the loss of a parent, you might say something like, "I'm so sorry. I lost a parent, too, and I know it's very painful." Encouraging emotions involves making validating and empathizing statements as are appropriate to the setting.

Here is an example of how you might do this in the real world. Assume you are negotiating with the gate agent at an airline terminal to bring your carry-on luggage aboard the plane. The agent thinks the bag is too big; you know from prior experience that it fits in the overhead bin and has been allowed on every flight before. You could get grumpy and tell the agent, "Well, every other time I've flown, they've let me on with it." If the agent is in a bad mood, all you have done is make this personal and invite her to exert her power. "Well, not this time," she might say, and you would find yourself having to go back to the ticket counter to check in your luggage. You might even miss your flight!

Instead, you could try using validation and empathy to encourage the agent's expression of frustration and fatigue. You might say, "I'm really sorry to have to trouble you over this. I'll bet it's been a busy day today." The agent might say, "You aren't kidding. It's been a total zoo around here today." You then might add, "And everyone hasn't been exactly patient and polite, right?" The agent might then look at you appreciatively and say, "Oh, don't get me started." At this point, is the agent feeling better about her interaction with you? Yes. You then might add, "I can put this in that measuring bin over there, but I know it fits. I've done it before." She then might say, "Oh, don't worry about it. I'll take your word for it." A seemingly intractable battle of wills has been avoided by the simple but powerful technique of encouraging and validating the other negotiator's emotions.

You can see that the strategic negotiator has a variety of ways he or she can manage and respond to difficult and challenging situations in any negotiation. The key to doing so effectively is the same as for all of negotiating: Manage or be managed.

Common Challenges in Business Negotiations

When it comes to business negotiations, size does not matter. Large and small businesses encounter and overcome difficulties common to both. The following are some of the most frequent challenges that arise in business negotiations and how clever negotiators deal with them.

The Angry Customer

On a particularly busy Monday morning, a customer approaches you in the cosmetics aisle of your drugstore as you are taking inventory and ordering new stock. You have had a terrible morning; one of your clerks called in sick, you are already short-handed, you have deliveries in the back of the store that need to be stocked, and there is a growing line at the check-out stand. The customer appears agitated and, without introducing herself or waiting for you to finish the entry you are making into your computerized inventory device, she brusquely asks, "Are you the manager?" You reply, "I am. What can I do for you?" She proceeds to berate you about the long line at the checkout stand and the mistakes that were made with filling her prescription. This is an important moment for your business. Your immediate internal reaction is to tell her to go jump in the lake.

But you have read this book, you are managing your internal reaction, and you realize that you need an ongoing relationship with each customer in order for your business to remain profitable and grow. "I'm sorry you've had to wait this morning, we're short-handed. Tell me about your prescription; it's important for me that every customer's order be properly filled." She tells you that this is the third time that the pharmacy has confused her name with that of her sister across town, and each time the staff has billed the wrong insurance, which causes the prescription to be rejected by the insurance company. This has resulted in a delay getting the prescription filled in addition to frustrating the customer. You thank the customer for pointing out the problem to you, and you tell her that you will get her name and insurance information and make sure that a special notice is placed at the pharmacy desk to attempt to avoid the problem in the future. "I hope that helps," you might say. The customer seems satisfied and thanks you. You take the extra step of personally taking care of her order at the checkout stand so she does not have to wait.

The odds are very good you have saved a customer. You have also discovered a systemic problem with your business that could be upsetting other customers. With some exceptions, the angry customer is experiencing frustrated expectations—the service or product she receives differs from that which she expects. This is a warning bell for the business. Whenever you have an angry customer, go below the line and find out what is happening before you do anything else. You might need to use cooperative negotiating techniques to avoid losing business. Whatever else you do, do not ignore or become angry with the customer before you find out what is going on, as this is how businesses lose customers. Cooperative negotiating techniques keep customers.

The Purchasing Deadline

An equipment, materials, or supplies distributor sales representative may insist that you make your purchase by a certain deadline or you will lose either a discount or the chance to buy at all. Perhaps the sales representative is being honest with you. More often than not, however, the urgency has to do with pressure being put upon the sales representative to make a specific quota or sales target at that time. Time deadlines are a common sales technique to close deals. If you do not have a pressing need for the equipment, materials, or supplies, you can easily tell the sales representative that you are not ready to order and to check back with you next month.

If, however, you do need to make the purchase, you must respond to the time deadline strategically. For example, you might tell the sales representative that you are looking at some other suppliers who are more flexible on the timing of the purchase. This is responding to a tactic with a tactic. If the time deadline is artificial, the sales representative is likely to respond that his company will work with you on the timing of your order by keeping the discount open or the products available. Another approach is to tell the sales representative that you really like dealing with his company, but that the time deadline technique does not work with you, and invite a different, more cooperative approach focused on when you need the product. This is responding to a tactic by identifying it and negotiating process.

> **Negotiating Tip**
>
> Successful businesses strategically use both competitive and cooperative negotiating approaches to maximize profit.

If, by chance, the time deadline is real, you will have to make a decision about what to do. Do you buy now or pass? The point is to know what your needs are and your time frame is before the negotiation and plan accordingly. Just understand that the time deadline is frequently used as a tactic to impart a sense of urgency, manage expectations, and close deals.

Dealing With Intimidation

You own a retail flower shop. You are preparing an order for 50 arrangements to be delivered to a restaurant for a wedding. You have never worked with this customer before. Three days before the delivery date, the restaurant owner calls you in a panic. He needs the arrangements delivered a day earlier because his clients want to begin advance decorating of the banquet room. These are very wealthy clients, the restaurant owner says, so he assumes you can comply. You cannot, you tell him. You have extra help working with you to meet the existing deadline, and you will deliver the arrangements early on the agreed date. The restaurant owner tells you that if you cannot comply, "I'm not paying you a dime. Understood?"

This is a regrettably common situation for small businesses. What do you do? Remember, think strategically. Do you have something the customer needs? Apparently so, because he is attempting to intimidate you into delivering it early. Thus, although he is not being very nice about it, he has signaled to you that early delivery has value to him. Treat the threat as an invitation to a new negotiation. You should be thinking at this moment: Can I deliver the flowers early and if so, what can I get for doing so? You might then respond, "We've never worked together before, but threatening me is no way to get me to do anything. I would need to stay here all night with my crew and pay them overtime to do this. That means we will need to change the agreed price. If you need these tomorrow, I'll do it, but the price is $X, and I will need it on delivery."

Every crisis presents at least the possibility of an opportunity. That is how successful business owners turn lemons into lemonade when they negotiate.

Responding to Silence

A colleague of ours tells a tale of how a negotiation professional can be out-maneuvered. She was contacted by the manager of a nonprofit organization about conducting a negotiation training course for its employees. Our colleague was grateful for the call. The prospective client asked our colleague how much she charged for a two-day program. Our colleague said, "$2,000 per day." There was silence on the phone. What do you think happened during this pause? Our colleague filled the empty space with talk. "If that's too much for your organization, I can do it for $1,700 per day." Silence. "If that won't work, how about $1,500?" The manager said, "Okay." Our colleague was conducting the training session some months later when the topic of tactics came up. One of the students said that the manager used that tactic all the time, and it was amazing how she got vendors to charge less for their services. Our colleague realized she had been worked by a professional. She wondered why she was teaching negotiation skills to these people when they were already learning from an expert.

In certain cultures, silence is a sign of respectful and thoughtful consideration of what has been said. Some Native American societies have this view of silence. In some instances, however, silence is being effectively used by experienced negotiators to extract concessions without giving up anything. The key to dealing with silence is silence itself. If the other negotiator grows silent in response to a proposal, be patient and silent. Remember, she who speaks first gives up too much. It may be hard to do this, but self-discipline is essential to strategic negotiating.

Negotiations may involve a variety of difficult moments you will need to strategically manage. We have explored how you might respond to tactics, negative behaviors, and strong emotions. Now we will look at how strategic negotiators put all of their knowledge and skills together to negotiate better deals.

Key Points to Remember: Chapter 4

1. Difficult moments in negotiating: emotions, tactics, or uncooperative behaviors.

2. The key to dealing with difficult moments: identify, assess, and strategically respond.

3. Responding to tactics: ignore, tactic back, or confront and negotiate process.

4. Dealing with strong emotions: ignore, discourage, or encourage and manage.

5. Strategic management of emotional moments: empathy, validation, and rapport.

CHAPTER 5

Putting Theory into Practice

Strategic Negotiating in Action

You can study negotiation a long time, but at some point you must put your knowledge into action. This is the hard part, but it can also be fun. If there is one main point to this book it is this: Those who fear negotiating are afraid not of the other negotiator, but of themselves. We do not fear negotiating because of what the other negotiator will do to us, but because of what we might do to ourselves by not strategically managing our negotiations. Don't be afraid to be the driver; not only can you get to your destination, but you just might enjoy the journey.

Preparing to Negotiate

Some negotiations are impromptu affairs, others present the opportunity for careful study and preparation. For example, if you are traveling in a foreign country, and you go to a market, you will have very little opportunity to learn about the actual cost of and the demand for that ceramic vase you have your eye on. Your lack of information cannot be remedied by much, if any, preparation. Therefore, your strategic management of the negotiation will be on the fly. You will send and receive signals during the negotiation that will give you limited, but important, information to guide you. You will have to put up with a high degree of uncertainty created by the lack of information. No amount of preparation will eliminate that environment. Still, you can do well in the negotiation by strategically managing yourself in an environment of uncertainty.

More frequently, you will have time to prepare for the negotiation. There is no single or best way to prepare for a negotiation. The following are suggestions about some basic things you can do to effectively prepare for any negotiation.

Determine Your Objective

What do you need out of the negotiation? A salary of a certain amount? A specific price for a home? A purchase price for a business and its good will? A specific amount of cash in your pocket in the settlement of a lawsuit? An end to the barking of your neighbor's dog? Certain property in a marital dissolution? Inventory of appliances at a specific cost? Every good negotiator has a clear idea of what she needs to achieve in the negotiation before the discussions begin.

An effective strategic negotiator also knows the difference between "needs" and "wants." Remember, an effective negotiator trying to maximize value in a competitive negotiation will keep dancing well after she can reach an agreement by saying "yes." While you may identify what you need in the negotiation, if you are in the competitive environment, you must also identify what you want to get out of the deal above and beyond your needs. By doing this, you may achieve a better deal. Businesses judge the relative success of their sales professionals by comparing the deals they achieve. The sales professionals who consistently achieve more value in their negotiations are judged more favorably than those who achieve less value.

On the CD-ROM accompanying this book, you will find forms entitled "Negotiation Strategy Assessment Tool" and "Negotiation Preparation Checklist." In preparing for any negotiation, use these forms to figure out what you need, what you want, and how you will map out your moves to achieve as much as you can in the negotiation. The objective is the destination to which you must drive safely. Your negotiating strategy is dictated by your objective.

> **Negotiating Tip**
>
> In preparing to negotiate, determine your objectives: what you want and what you need.

Know the Market

Whether you are buying a car or hiring an employee, you should always know the market for the good or service about which you are negotiating. You can acquire this knowledge in a variety of ways. Years of experience in a particular business, coupled with regular study of trends in that business, is one way of knowing your market. Internet research about the demand for and inventory of a certain product—a car, for example—is another way of learning the market. If you are in a foreign market place, cruising all of the vendors' stalls to see the inventory and competition is another way to learn the market. If you are selling lumber or appliances or toasters, review historical data about sales. There are countless forms of research, but the ultimate goal is the same. Gain as much information as you can about the supply and demand for the good or service about which you will be negotiating.

Determine Your Bottom Line

Every good negotiator knows the point beyond which he will not go. This is the point where you must be prepared to walk away from the table. Effectively determining this point, however, is a tricky business. Sometimes the bottom line is not realistically obtainable in the negotiation or by any other means. If the bottom line does not reflect reality, the negotiator sets himself up for failure. For example, you might want that brand new luxury car for $5,000, but it is not realistic to make that your bottom line. A bottom line of $35,000 for the car might be more realistic in light of the demand for and supply of the car in the marketplace.

Thus, in order to determine an effective and useful bottom line, the negotiator has to evaluate her options away from the table, i.e., in the event no deal is reached. Fisher and Ury, the authors of *Getting to Yes*, popularized a way for negotiators to objectively evaluate their alternatives away from the table, which they referred to as "BATNA" and "WATNA." To these, we and others have added a third term, "MLATNA." The following is an explanation of these terms and how they assist negotiators in figuring out their bottom lines.

Best Alternative to Negotiated Agreement (BATNA)

Any deal you might achieve in a negotiation must be compared with the kind of deal you might obtain some other way (e.g., by negotiating with someone else or going to court). In that way, you can compare the benefits of reaching an agreement in the negotiation with the benefits of not reaching agreement. Your BATNA is the best possible outcome if you do not reach an agreement in this negotiation. What will happen? This requires a certain degree of educated guessing. In the commercial world, your BATNA might be the price for which you can buy a certain product or service from someone other than the person with whom you are negotiating. Or your BATNA might be the price you could receive for your product or service from another buyer. In the legal world, your BATNA usually is the best possible outcome you could achieve in court if everything goes your way.

All potential deals in a negotiation must be measured in comparison to one's BATNA. Of course, your BATNA is only useful to the extent that you can predict what will

> **Negotiating Tip**
>
> To determine your bottom line, you must accurately estimate your best, worst, and most likely alternatives away from the table.

happen in the future. In some situations, that projection is an educated guess. In others, it is a sheer gamble, a roll of the dice. In every instance, you must try to make a realistic estimate of your BATNA. Good negotiators estimate their BATNAs conservatively, not overly optimistically, and they base their projections on objective information, not fantasy.

Worst Alternative to Negotiated Agreement (WATNA)

A negotiator would be foolish to measure the options achievable in the negotiation against the best-case scenario if no deal is reached. The best-case scenario frequently proves inaccurate. Often, things do not go as planned. You might not be able to get those tires at the same or better price at another dealer. You might not get a judgment in your favor if you go to court. You might not get a higher salary or better benefits by quitting your job and finding another.

So the strategic negotiator must measure the benefits of negotiating an agreement against not only the BATNA, but against the worst-case scenario if no deal is reached—the WATNA. In some instances, the WATNA is not so bad. For example, if you are purchasing tires for your car, your WATNA might be buying them from another dealer in town at the same price. You could stop negotiating with one tire seller knowing that the worst that can happen is that you will get the tires from another seller at the same price. You can afford to wait for a better price. You have options.

What if you are driving to Las Vegas at four in the morning, and you get a flat tire in Barstow? Your only option for replacing the tire is Sneaky Eddie's Tires, and he's charging you twice the normal price for replacing the tire. You have to be in Las Vegas by 8:00 a.m. for an important meeting. Your WATNA in that instance is missing your meeting. That is not good. Your BATNA is waiting until other tire stores open in Barstow and trying to get a better deal, which means you will still miss your meeting. Not good. You will do the deal with Sneaky Eddie because your WATNA is so much worse than your BATNA in that situation. Sometimes, the deal at the table is acceptable because it is less bad than your WATNA, i.e., you are minimizing loss or making the best of a bad situation. This occurs frequently in the business world, when cutting one's losses is the best decision the negotiator can make.

Most Likely Alternative to Negotiated Agreement (MLATNA)

What negotiators most frequently do is try to estimate what the most probable outcome will be if they do not reach a deal in the negotiation. Typically, one must study the market, know the competition, evaluate jury verdicts, study past economic performance, and do other types of research to accurately gauge probabilities of future events. If you have received a private commitment to purchase a commodity at a specific price, your MLATNA is reasonably certain. If your lawyer has litigated your type of lawsuit before and never lost, your MLATNA is less certain, but your comfort level with the uncertainty of what will happen in court is greater.

Assigning probabilities to future events is inherently speculative, so the degree of certainty or uncertainty to one's MLATNA must be evaluated with objectivity, precision, and care. Typically, the best way to gauge one's MLATNA is to have as much objective information as possible about the alternatives to the deal that is achievable in the negotiation. What have juries done in cases like yours in this court in recent times? What is your lawyer's track record in cases like yours in this court in recent times? What is the supply of and demand for this product at this time in your market? What is the current market value for the product in your area? How many other businesses are you competing with concerning the sale or purchase of this product or service? What is the current availability in your area of employees with the skill and experience you need in this position?

Avoid wishful thinking or over-estimating your chances of getting a better deal away from the table. Accurately estimating one's MLATNA must be done with one's eyes wide open about the realities of reaching a better deal away from the table. The less you know about your options away from the table, the less reliable your estimate of your MLATNA will be. Blind guesses are bad for business. Projections based on reliable, objective information

FIGURE 5-1. **Negotiation Outcome Analysis**

	Best Alternative (BATNA)	Worst Alternative (WATNA)	Most Likely Alternative (MLATNA)	Today
PAY	$0 (Win)	−$150,000 (Lose)	−$30,000-50,000	−$30,000
Less Costs	−$25,000	−$25,000	−$25,000	−$10,000
NET	−$25,000	−$175,000	−$55,000-85,000	−$40,000

make for good business decisions. When in doubt, estimate your MLATNA conservatively; that is, guess that the options away from the table are not as good as you think they are.

After you have evaluated your BATNA, WATNA and MLATNA, then you should determine your bottom line—the point at which you will walk away from the table. This involves comparing your estimate of your best, worst, and most probable options for meeting your needs away from the table as opposed to continuing the negotiation. Some negotiators find it helpful to list the BATNA, WATNA, and MLATNA on a sheet of paper as they are considering whether to continue negotiating or not. Figure 5-1 illustrates how an employer might make such a list concerning the negotiation of the settlement of a lawsuit brought against him by a former employee.

In the example in Figure 5-1, the employer lists his BATNA, WATNA, and MLATNA, along with the costs of going to trial. The employer then compares those estimated payouts with the amount of money for which he can settle the case at the negotiation. Notice that the legal costs the employer has incurred at the time of the negotiation are less than those that will occur by the conclusion of a trial. The employer must then look at the probabilities and the net expenditures and make an objective decision about how best to manage the risk of the lawsuit. Does the employer wish to gamble on winning at trial, which still leaves him $25,000 in the hole for legal expenses, or pay

> **Negotiating Tip**
>
> Be pessimistic and flexible, not optimistic and rigid, in determining your BATNA, WATNA, and MLATNA.

$30,000 to settle the case now, for a total expense of the lawsuit of $40,000? Is a best-case scenario of saving $15,000 by going to trial worth spending $25,000 to get that result? Is paying a total of $40,000 in the lawsuit now better than having to pay $55,000–$175,000 by the end of trial if the employer loses? Listing one's BATNA, WATNA, and MLATNA is an effective way of objectively making the decision about whether to continue negotiating or walk away from the table. Businesses use this form of rational decision making every day to try to achieve their BATNAs while trying to avoid their WATNAs.

A word of caution, though: be flexible. You may find that the negotiation reveals values you had not anticipated previously, thus causing you to be less rigid about your bottom line. There may be reasons to stay at the table, so long as you are achieving the value you need from the negotiation. You might hold out for a better deal, but the uncertainty and risk might be unacceptably high in comparison to your need to close the deal now. Good strategic negotiators understand that they need to be open-minded about achieving their needs and interests in a negotiation. After all, openmindedness and flexibility are keys to the communication and creativity that are characteristic of cooperative negotiating. Flexibility is also critical to the exchange of concessions that closes deals in competitive negotiating.

Know Your Negotiating Partner

What did the owner of the football team in Chapter 1 have over the player's agent in that negotiation? Superior knowledge of his negotiating partner. The owner learned about the agent's behavior before the negotiation, and he fashioned his approach accordingly. The owner agreed too quickly, knowing that would embolden the agent to ask for more. You can learn about your negotiating partner in a variety of ways, including prior dealings with that person, speaking to others who have negotiated with that person, doing some internet research, and by studying the communications you have received from that person for signals.

For example, if you are interested in possibly buying a home, you might go to the open house. There, you are likely to meet the seller's listing agent. To gain information about that person's negotiating style, after the usual social preliminaries and taking a look around, you might say, "How long has the house been on the market?" If the agent gives you the accurate answer (you might have learned this from the internet in advance), you then could say, "Why are the sellers selling?" The agent might say the sellers have found another home, which tells you that they might be eager to sell, which might mean they will be flexible on price. You can learn a great deal about the other negotiator through this kind of preliminary fishing for information. It can be done politely and socially while establishing rapport. Great negotiators do this all the time.

Business owners gain information from the signals that their customers give them. For example, if you own a retail computer hardware and software store, you can learn whether a prospective customer is eager to purchase ("Do you have a computer system now?" or "When were you thinking of purchasing a new system?"), how much they are willing to pay ("What is your price range?"), and whether they are competitive or cooperative negotiators (Do they answer or evade your questions? How do they answer your questions?).

Anticipate What Your Negotiating Partner Might Need or Value

In the course of learning about your negotiating partner, you should try to learn as much as you can about what he values in the negotiation. This will help you fashion a negotiating strategy that delivers value to your negotiating partner in addition to achieving the value you seek in the negotiation. Also, understanding the relative value the other negotiator gives to certain deal

> **Negotiating Tip**
>
> Before you begin negotiating, learn everything you can about the other negotiator, including whether he or she is cooperative or competitive.

points will help you identify your sources of power or leverage in the negotiation. The tire shop owner in Barstow has a really good sense of the importance to you of replacing your flat tire, and he will raise his price accordingly. As discussed in Chapter 2, linkage is a way that negotiators get value by providing value. We used the example of a car dealer who provides a buyer with a low monthly payment that accommodates the buyer's minimal cash flow. Of course, the car dealer makes a bigger profit than if the buyer could pay more per month in exchange for a lower sale price.

There are many ways you can learn what is important to your negotiating partner. You can do market research as discussed above. You can fish for information before and during your negotiation. You can watch for signals of eagerness or hesitancy during the negotiation. In Chapter 2, we discussed how you gain such information from the timing and size of the concessions the other negotiator makes in competitive negotiating. If you and the other negotiator are engaged in cooperative negotiating, you can discuss your underlying interests and needs openly and frankly. There are myriad ways in which the negotiators can gain information about what they each value.

Determine Your Opening and Fallback Offers

Strategic negotiators know before the negotiation what their opening and subsequent moves are going to be. In this way, strategic negotiating is very much like the game of chess; you plan your moves based upon what your negotiating partner's moves are likely to be. At least have the first several moves planned out, and you can adjust as the negotiation progresses. In Chapter 2, we discussed how competitive negotiators aim high and negotiate down to maximize value at the table. Asking for more value at the beginning of the negotiation usually results in getting more value at the end of the negotiation. Also, remember that in competitive negotiating, the end-point usually is the mid-point between the first two reasonable offers. Why not make the end-point closer to your side of the table by planning your opening moves accordingly?

For example, some negotiators find it helpful to map out their anticipated negotiating moves on a sheet of paper, which might look something like this:

I offer	$100,000	My bottom line = $70,000
She offers	$50,000	Would like to get = $75,000
I offer	$90,000	
She offers	$60,000	
I offer	$85,000	
(and so on...)		

Mapping out your moves is a good way of creating a negotiating game plan that permits the dance to unfold in a strategic way if you are engaged in a competitive negotiation. No matter how well you plan your moves, however, you must be prepared to adjust the game plan depending on how the negotiation progresses. In the example above, if you open at $100,000, and the other negotiator offers $40,000, rather than $50,000, you will have to rethink your planned offer of $90,000. You might need to counter at $95,000 if your bottom line is $70,000 because the other negotiator started lower than you anticipated. The best negotiators adjust the game plan if the negotiation progresses other than as anticipated. The Negotiating Strategy Assessment Tool in the CD accompanying this book has a space in the form for mapping out your opening and fallback moves.

Determine Whether You Will Be Cooperative, Competitive, or Both

It can be difficult to decide whether you should use a cooperative approach, a competitive approach, or a bit of both. Here are some simple guidelines you might consider in making that choice:

Remember Axelrod's Theory: Begin Cooperatively

One of the great misperceptions about cooperative and competitive negotiating approaches is that they are mutually exclusive. They are not. Effective strategic negotiators can achieve a competitive objective (acquiring something of value from someone willing to give it up) using a cooperative approach (soft on the people, hard on the issue). Your mother may have told you, "You can catch more flies with honey than with vinegar." That is the idea. You can negotiate competitively, but do so in a way that is easy on the other negotiator so he will want to part with value. For example, when you walk into luxury car dealerships, they ooze "soft on the people." They will be polite, somewhat deferential, offer you a latte, and let you roam a bit before inviting any questions. This is an overtly cooperative tactic. Underlying that cooperation, however, is a competitive negotiating approach. You will pay more for that kind of attention, the quality of the car, and the prestige of the brand.

> ### Negotiating Tip
>
> Decide beforehand whether you are going to negotiate cooperatively, competitively, or a bit of both.

In other instances, you will want to identify those aspects of the negotiation that are likely to be competitive (carving up a fixed pie) and those that are ripe for cooperation (expanding the pie by focusing on mutually shared interests). For example, in every negotiation between an employer and a prospective employee, there are elements of both competition and cooperation. The competitive part of the negotiation involves compensation and benefits. The employer wants to minimize that number and the employee wants to maximize that number. Both negotiators, however, understand that the focus of the negotiation is the underlying working relationship. The employer does not want to be too competitive, otherwise the employee will be unhappy and seek other employment; the employee does not want to be too competitive and either lose the job or undermine the employer's trust in her. Thus, both negotiators must plan for how they will handle the cooperative and competitive parts of the negotiation before it actually begins.

Be Competitive with a Competitive Negotiating Partner

If you walk into an automobile dealership, it does not matter how nice, mellow, low-key, and cooperative the salesperson may seem. This is a competitive negotiation at its core. The salesperson is trying to maximize and you should be trying to minimize the amount of money you will pay. Select a competitive strategy before you walk into the showroom. Fish for information with strategic questions designed to learn whether this car has been selling well, how many such cars they have in stock, what kind of incentives the dealer or the manufacturer has on the car in which you are interested, whether the dealer is willing to beat any other dealer's price. There is no relationship you want to preserve. You want to get the best price on the car you want, period.

Be clear why you are selecting a competitive strategy and implement it. You are on a mission to maximize value in competitive negotiating. You can be pleasant about it, that is "soft on the people," but you have an objective to accomplish. It is strictly business, nothing personal. That is exactly how the salesperson and the dealership will be approaching the negotiation. This is also how businesses pay less for supplies and equipment, and are paid more for the goods and services they sell. You are in business to maximize profit in an honorable and honest way that preserves the good will of your business. Competitive negotiating is a way to do just that.

Select a Cooperative Technique Where Ongoing Interaction Is Unavoidable or Future Cooperation Is Valuable

When two neighbors are in conflict over a noisy dog, the trimming of trees, or the parking of cars, they may assume that there is no relationship they wish to preserve. Instead, they may perceive that they are completely independent of each other and either indifferent or antagonistic toward each other's needs, thus making the resolution of their conflict through negotiation difficult. Yet, there is value to both harmony and cooperation between them. There would be less stress, more peace, and greater enjoyment of their respective homes in the absence of conflict and with the advent of coexistence and cooperation between them.

> **Negotiating Tip**
>
> To preserve or build a relationship, cooperative negotiating is the best approach.

Thus, while the two neighbors might take an aggressive competitive approach to negotiating a resolution of their conflict ("stop your dog from barking, or I'll call the police"), the most effective means of reaching agreement is through use of a cooperative negotiating approach, which focuses on finding solutions for mutual gain. That is because the neighbors share a common boundary, they live next door to each other, and their future interactions are unavoidable. They have no choice but to recognize and serve their underlying shared interest in harmonious coexistence. Using the three steps of the cooperative negotiating process, starting with being "soft on the people, hard on the issues," will yield a more durable solution for both negotiators in this instance.

A similar principle applies to business negotiations. A furniture retailer enjoys a competitive and cooperative negotiating relationship with her largest wholesale distributor. On one hand, the retailer wants to pay the distributor as little as possible for her inventory. On the other hand, the retailer needs the distributor to provide high quality merchandise on a predictable and regular basis. Without inventory, the retailer will have reduced sales. The distributor has a similar relationship with the retailer; the distributor benefits by selling as many units as possible, and that is achieved by maximizing retail outlet relationships. On the other hand, the distributor wants to sell each unit for as much money as possible to maximize profits.

The strategic negotiator recognizes when it is in her best interest to adopt a cooperative negotiating approach as opposed to a competitive one. Where ongoing interaction is unavoidable, or where cooperation is valuable to both negotiators, the strategic negotiator selects a cooperative approach, all the while paying careful attention to Axelrod's Theory of avoiding exploitation. Strategic self-management is the key to effectively employing cooperative negotiating techniques where there is conflict or elements of competition. The best negotiators do this very successfully to reach great deals in challenging or seemingly impossible situations.

Once the strategic negotiator has figured out her game plan, it is game time. That is when the plan must be implemented.

Beginning the Negotiation

Now the fun can begin, but there is a fundamental strategic question that must be answered first. Who makes the opening offer that gets the negotiation going?

There are differing schools of thought on the answer to this question. One school of thought suggests that the seller always makes the opening offer, and this is logical. A seller of goods wants to attract as many buyers as possible at the highest price. But the seller competes with other sellers of the same product, so the price has to be low enough to attract enough buyers. In this common situation, the seller makes the opening offer for a sound strategic reason: She might not have a negotiation at all unless she does so.

> **Negotiating Tip**
>
> Making the opening offer can be powerful, but letting the other negotiator do so can be equally advantageous: it gives you important information.

Still, there are situations where it is strategically advantageous for the seller *not* to make the first offer. Remember the seller of the mint condition collector's car in Chapter 1? The seller in that situation, who has an eager buyer approach him before he places the sales price on the car, might strategically decide to invite the buyer to make the first offer. He might be pleasantly surprised and the buyer might offer more than he anticipated.

Whenever an automobile dealer puts a sticker price on the car, that is the opening offer. The buyer has no option but to make the responsive offer. And why does the dealer enjoy an advantage in making this opening offer? Remember Chapter 2: The opening offer can manage the expectations of the responding negotiator and cause a magnetic pull effect that benefits the seller. There can be great power in making the opening offer for this reason alone. The key is knowing when that power exists, as opposed to conceding too much by making the opening offer.

Therefore, the strategic negotiator always considers whether he is in a position to make the first offer and, if so, whether it is strategically advantageous to do so. You might consider making the first offer where:

- the other negotiator has not made the first offer
- you do not enjoy a position of power or leverage in the negotiation
- the other negotiator is aggressively competitive and you anticipate her opening offer might be extreme or offensive
- you have a good estimate of the other negotiator's BATNA, WATNA, or MLATNA
- you have credible information about the other negotiator's underlying needs and interests
- you want to manage the other negotiator's expectations at the beginning.

You may wish to consider letting the other negotiator make the opening offer where:

- you do not have a good estimate of the other negotiator's BATNA, WATNA, or MLATNA
- the market for the good or service is uncertain
- you enjoy a position of power or leverage in the negotiation
- you lack credible information about the other negotiator's underlying needs and interests
- the other negotiator appears cooperative
- the other party is a less skilled negotiator
- you do not know whether you will concede too much by making the opening offer.

It may seem counter-intuitive to suggest that the strategic negotiator should refrain from making the opening offer whenever he lacks an informed estimate of the other negotiator's BATNA, WATNA, and MLATNA, but to make the first offer when you have such information. There is, however, sound reasoning behind this recommendation. When you have a good idea of whether the other negotiator can get a better or worse deal if she does not reach agreement with you, you can use that information to target the opening offer so that it will be attractive. Also, you can feel confident you are not offering too great a concession by opening first because you have a good idea of whether the other negotiator can do better or worse negotiating with someone else. For example, in the classic car negotiation, if you know that another seller down the street is offering a similar make and model of car in a similar condition, you might want to make the first offer to induce the other negotiator to buy your car.

This dynamic is reversed when you lack information about the other negotiator's best, worst, and most likely alternatives to doing the deal with you. In that environment of uncertainty—for example, when you are shopping at a flea market in a foreign country—you do not know whether your opening offer is too high or too low in relation to what the other negotiator can get if he holds out for a deal with someone else. In that situation, you gain information by inviting the other negotiator to make the first offer. "What do you really want for this vase?" Then, if the seller reduces the price, you know that he is eager to sell, thus signaling a sizeable dance floor. Letting the other negotiator make the opening offer gives you very useful information in this situation.

When phrasing your opening offer, remember Chapter 2: Choose flexible language for an extreme opening offer, and firm language for a reasonable opening offer. The predictability of competitive bargaining is such that you may pre-ordain the end-point by how you begin. And with cooperative negotiating, as discussed in Chapter 3, you can only create the rapport and trust necessary to reach a deal by using language that is "soft on the people, hard on the issue."

When to Walk Away

Many negotiators try to put a deal together even if it turns out to be wrong for either or both parties. A competitive negotiator may be perfectly pleased with a bad deal for the other negotiator who is cooperative. Worse, two negotiators may put together a deal that is terrible because it does not meet either of their needs as well as doing something else or because it will fall apart before the ink is dry. Sometimes, the best thing to do is nothing, no deal. That may be better than putting a bad deal together. In such instances, walking away from a deal is sound strategic thinking.

In other instances, walking away is a competitive tactic designed to extract an important concession. When you negotiate a car deal or you are at the flea market, the most powerful thing you can do to achieve the value you need may be to walk away, or at least to threaten to do so. Of course, this competitive tactic requires a reasonably good estimate of your BATNA, WATNA and MLATNA. For walking away or the threat of walking away to have power, your BATNA, WATNA, and MLATNA together must be very good. If you are confident you can purchase the same car or trinket elsewhere for a better price, walking away makes great sense. And this powerful move can force the

Negotiating Tip

To effectively use the power of walking away, know your alternatives away from the table.

seller to reduce the offer if he really wants to sell the product. Effective negotiators use this competitive tactic all the time to get the best deals.

Of course, the risk one assumes in walking away is that there will be no deal. Additionally, if the other negotiator has accurately gauged her BATNA, WATNA and MLATNA, and you have not, you will get even less favorable terms if you go back to that same negotiator after walking away. It is obvious at that point that the other negotiator's power has increased and that yours has diminished. So walking away is a science best employed when your BATNA, WATNA and MLATNA are, in balance, much better than the deal on the table, and when the other negotiator's BATNA, WATNA and MLATNA are much worse.

Closing the Deal

The strategic negotiator knows how to close the deal. Closing is a science and an art because it depends on persuading the other negotiator that he has received all the concessions possible and that one of two things is left to do: reach agreement or end the negotiation without agreement. There are many views on closing effectively. Some urge slick, pressure tactics for closing. "Killer Closing Techniques to Unleash Your Inner Shark," might be a title for this school of helpful advice. Others urge less flashy but nonetheless effective techniques common in sales and marketing, including follow-up calls, long-term relationship building, and the like. We believe that there are no tricks or gimmicks to closing, simply techniques that vary with the situation.

We take a holistic approach to the moment when an agreement is reached at the conclusion of a negotiation. It happens when both negotiators are convinced the agreement meets their needs and interests, and when they believe that they cannot find a better deal elsewhere. Therefore, the key to closing is fulfilling these twin expectations.

Both negotiators are likely to feel that the exchange of concessions or proposals has ended and that they have achieved the best terms possible when the following occur:

- the competitive negotiating dance has run its course (i.e., it has not been short-circuited)
- attempts to gain additional concessions have been unsuccessful
- both negotiators' BATNAs are not as good as the deal on the table
- both negotiators' WATNAs are worse than the deal on the table
- both negotiators' MLATNAs are similar in value to or worse than the deal on the table
- both negotiators' core needs and interests are fulfilled by the deal on the table
- both negotiators wish to avoid losing the deal on the table (i.e., the net benefits of the deal exceed the net costs of the deal)
- at least one of the negotiators feels he or she has "won" the negotiation.

Therefore, the strategic negotiator closes the deal by managing the process so that she feels that no further gains can be achieved and that the deal meets her needs. Most importantly, the strategic negotiator must manage the process so that the *other negotiator* feels the same way. The management of expectations and the use of signals discussed in Chapter 2, as well as the techniques of cooperative negotiating discussed in Chapter 3, will close deals if employed wisely and patiently. The following techniques are specific methods that strategic negotiators use to close deals.

Time Deadlines

A paradox of negotiating is that a negotiator's ability to make a decision can be helped or hindered by time. In some instances, too much time encourages the negotiators to delay making a decision. If the delay serves the purpose of better informing the negotiators about their BATNAs, WATNAs, and MLATNAs, then it has served a strategic purpose. If, however, the negotiators are simply putting off making a decision, the results can be counter-productive.

Correspondingly, too little time can impair intelligent decision making. A common aggressive, competitive negotiating tactic is for one negotiator to impose a unilateral deadline by which the other negotiator is to make a decision. Frequently, negotiators who enjoy a superior position of leverage or power use this tactic effectively. Other times, a reasonable time deadline can help the negotiators to make an informed decision rather than simply putting it off to another day.

Examples of effective time deadlines in the business world include commercial advertisements containing phrases such as "Limited Time Offer," or "Sale Ends On _____," or "Offer Expires On _____," or "While Supplies Last!" Construction professionals place deadlines in which the developer or homeowner must accept a bid or proposal (e.g., 20 days, 30 days). Sales and marketing professionals offer volume discounts if purchases are made within a specific time. And the list goes on. Businesses of all shapes and sizes make effective use of time deadlines to get their customers or vendors to close deals.

Anchoring

As mentioned in Chapter 2, the effective negotiator uses psychology to frame his final offer as a gain for the other negotiator as opposed to a loss. We used the example of a labor/collective bargaining negotiation between a manufacturer and a union, but anchoring can be used to encourage the other negotiator to cash in his chips and accept your last proposal. Frequently, an effective negotiator will summarize the gains the other negotiator has already achieved and can preserve by saying "yes" to the deal. This encourages the other negotiator to consider whether he wants to lose all that he has gained in order to achieve a little bit more in the deal.

For example, if you are a retailer of televisions, DVD players, and stereo equipment, you may be involved in a lengthy competitive negotiation with a major distributor concerning your purchase of a large volume of inventory. After many moves in the dance, you strategically decide upon a bottom-line price. You can use anchoring to close this deal, particularly if you enjoy a position of leverage. You might make your final, walk-away proposal this way: "We have spent a lot of time trying to work out a deal. I appreciate your company's willingness to work with us, and I think we have both made many concessions to try to make this happen. We have already offered 25 percent more for this inventory than we budgeted, and that is in an increasingly competitive business with shrinking profit margins. We want to make this work, and we are prepared to make a final investment in this deal. We will offer you what amounts to a 30 percent increase in our budgeted purchase allot-

> **Negotiating Tip**
>
> There are no gimmicks to closing the deal, but there are a wide variety of techniques for getting the other negotiator to say yes.

ment. We think that is more than fair, and we expect it to close the deal." Your choice of language may differ, but the point is the same: You are telling the other negotiator in a polite but firm way to cash in his chips.

Linkage

As we discussed in Chapter 2, sometimes the pie over which the parties are negotiating is too small and agreement becomes elusive. In these instances, experienced negotiators reach for value in other pies to link with the pie over which they are already negotiating. Examples of creative linkage include timing of payment, installment versus lump sum payments, interest rates and discounts, free services (e.g., storage, delivery), payment of closing costs in real estate deals, escrow periods, inclusion of furniture in a real estate purchase, and the list goes on. In the retail business, delayed payments, interest-free payments, and discounted service contracts are forms of linkage. Businesses use linkage in countless creative ways to close deals every day.

Brainstorming

Remember Chapter 3 and the creation of options for mutual gain? This is a key component of cooperative negotiating. Successful negotiators frequently close difficult deals by asking the other negotiator, "What if I could [fill in the blank with the other negotiator's unmet interest]? Could we do the deal then?" Sometimes the negotiators can brainstorm options for mutual gain at the end of a negotiation and come up with new ideas or previously discarded ideas that now seem more appealing. Another question that business negotiators ask to close deals through creative brainstorming is, "Do you have any ideas I haven't thought of to structure this deal in a way that works for both of us?" It is amazing what asking for ideas from the other negotiator can do to creatively close deals.

Saving an Important Concession to the End

An effective strategic negotiator knows that she should hold an important concession in reserve as a deal closer. Many deals are closed when the negotiator makes such a concession at the end of a long negotiation. A strategic negotiator may be perfectly willing to make the concession earlier, but he or she must be mindful of the importance of the other negotiator's satisfaction with the process of the negotiation and the deal. Strategic management of the negotiation process means tailoring your moves so that the other negotiator will do what you need him to do. Frequently, that means saving an important concession to the end so that the other negotiator can feel like the winner. This is particularly true in competitive negotiating.

Rapport and Persuasion

If you have established good rapport with the other negotiator, you can be very persuasive. If you are using a competitive technique and the other negotiator is inherently and non-strategically cooperative, rapport and persuasion are particularly effective. An articulate argument emphasizing the value of the deal being offered, particularly if it adequately meets the other negotiator's underlying interests, can close the deal very nicely. Particularly in cooperative negotiating, there comes a time when both negotiators need to be satisfied that they have achieved their objectives and that further negotiating might jeopardize the deal or their relationship. Rapport builds trust, and honest communication is the most persuasive.

The Soft Sell

Good salespeople know that not pushing and letting the buyer come to you can be a very effective technique in closing deals. For example, if you are selling new audio equipment at a dealership, you know that consumers are overwhelmed by the choices and pricing of the equipment by various dealers. You also know that they have been pestered at other stores to buy now. They will be reluctant to deal with you, but you can be low key and simply show

> **Negotiating Tip**
>
> The sophisticated negotiator knows when to push and when to back off in closing the deal.

them different options at various price ranges. You can also answer their questions and simply give them your card. You can act like you would like to take care of them, but that you are patient and will let them tell you when it is time. Consumers like this approach so much that they will frequently do the deal with a salesperson like this, sometimes at a higher price, than someone more pushy.

Walking Away

Whether you are competitively negotiating a car deal or the purchase of a trinket at a market, if the other negotiator stops making concessions after several rounds of exchanging offers, you can shrug and tell her that you will go elsewhere. Sometimes that statement alone can extract a further concession from the other negotiator. Sometimes it does not. Then, as you physically walk away, the other negotiator may come to you with another concession. Perhaps a day after you leave the automobile dealership, you will get a call from the salesperson. It all depends on the market for the product about which you are negotiating. Remember, walking away or the threat of doing so only works if your BATNA is really good, your WATNA is not so bad, and your MLATNA is better than the deal you are being offered.

Meeting the Other Negotiator's Interests and Needs

As we discussed in Chapter 3, cooperative negotiating is successful in creating mutually satisfying agreements. The other negotiator is more likely to accept the agreement if you have made a genuine attempt to address his underlying interests and meet his core needs. This, of course, takes good listening and patience; that is the only way you learn about the underlying interests of the other negotiator.

Make the Other Negotiator Feel Like a Winner

Effective business negotiators have learned that a little play acting can go a long way to closing a deal. There are times when you may wish to pretend that a concession you are making is particularly painful or difficult even if it is something you planned to do all along. You save such a move for the final act, and then top it with a little theater. "You have really worked me over. All right, I'll give you this, but all I have left is my dignity." Some variant of this performance can be very effective in satisfying the other negotiator's need to win the deal. It is okay to let the other negotiator feel like the winner.

Begin Writing Up the Deal

Many negotiators who are great closers bring the paperwork with them to the negotiation. As agreement is reached on several main points, they will bring out the agreement form and beginning filling in the necessary information. This creates momentum toward agreement. It is immediate, visual, and tangible. And it is highly successful in closing deals.

Strategic negotiators have countless ways that they close deals. Typically, however, deals are reached when the negotiators both believe that no further concessions are forthcoming, and that the deal meets their needs on some level. The key is managing the process so that you and the other negotiator get to that point. In negotiating, the destination is really the product of the journey.

The Durability of Agreements

Ultimately, both negotiators want an agreement that is lasting and durable; that is, one that will be performed. Sometimes agreements do not meet this test. They may fall apart after the negotiation, or there may be disagreements during the agreement's implementation. Typically, agreements fail because the negotiating process has not been managed effectively by either or both negotiators. Figure 5-2 shows three factors that lead to a durable agreement.

- *Procedural Satisfaction.* This occurs when the negotiation has been managed in a way that both parties feel they have achieved all gains possible, and that further negotiation runs the risk of creating impasse. The "dance" has not been short-circuited. The process has been managed in a way that is satisfying to both negotiators.
- *Psychological Satisfaction.* This occurs when the negotiators' underlying needs and interests have been met sufficiently by the negotiating process and the deal for them to feel "satisfied" on a psychological level. This element is critical to the durability of the agreement.
- *Substantive Satisfaction.* This occurs when the terms of the agreement meet the parties' underlying needs and interests, and both parties conclude that the net benefits of the agreement outweigh its net costs. The deal has to be psychologically satisfying for both negotiators on some level, otherwise there will be problems finalizing or implementing it.

FIGURE 5-2. **The Durability Triangle**

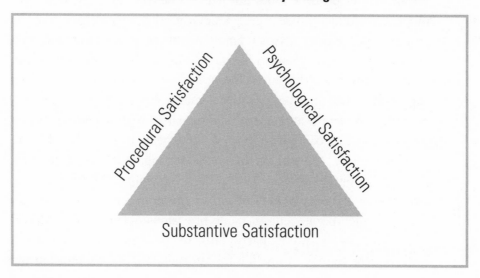

Successful negotiators know how to structure competitive negotiating so that the other negotiator feels like the winner in the end. When it is time to negotiate cooperatively, the successful negotiator works hard to meet the underlying needs and interests of the other negotiator by proposing options for mutual gain. The best negotiators understand and accept the three pillars of durable agreements, and they manage their negotiations accordingly. Closing is the end of a successfully managed negotiation process, not an end in itself. It is the product of strategic negotiating masterfully managed.

The Agreement: The Devil Is in the Details

When the parties reach agreement, there are a number of things they need to do.

- *Clarify the Terms.* Be clear about who is doing what, when, where, and how. Payment and performance terms should be clear. Deadlines should be clear.

- *Put It in Writing?* In most instances, an agreement does not need to be in writing in order to be a contract that is legally binding. In certain instances, a written agreement may not be necessary. For example, an agreement between family members concerning who will take care of certain chores probably does not need to be in writing. In some cultures, demanding a written agreement rather than a handshake could be an insult, particularly between family members. In all other instances, however, particularly concerning any commercial agreement, put it in writing! This makes the parties' rights and obligations crystal clear, and it provides a way that both parties demonstrate their shared commitment to abide by the agreement. Additionally, a written contract is easier to enforce in court than an oral agreement. It is much harder to avoid contractual obligations that are in writing; oral agreements simply invite disputes between the negotiators' memories of the deal.

- *Enforcement.* When lawyers draft agreements at the end of negotiations, they will incorporate enforcement provisions—clauses that address what happens if either party fails to perform his obligations. Enforcement terms can provide for attorney fees and expenses in the event of litigation, a dispute resolution provision such as mediation or arbitration in lieu of or prior to initiating litigation, a fixed penalty for non-performance (liquidated damages), a stipulated judgment in the event of default, acceleration of the balance due on a promissory note, foreclosure on secured collateral, and the list goes on. It is best to seek the advice of an attorney concerning any of these enforcement provisions because they contain legal wording that creates rights and responsibilities. Additionally, in many states, the wording of enforcement provisions of contracts must comply with certain laws, including the placement of certain language in the written agreement itself. Businesses are best advised to consult with a lawyer in the course of drafting important commercial agreements.

> **Negotiating Tip**
>
> The best deal in the world is worthless if you do not pay careful attention to detail in the closing stage.

A word of caution about enforcement provisions. In a real sense, they are a form of planning for failure. This is not a terribly optimistic way to conclude an agreement. Also, negotiating an enforcement provision (i.e., planning for what happens if either of the negotiators fails to perform), can turn a cooperative negotiation into a competitive one and kill the deal. So great care must be given to negotiating enforcement provisions. If concern is great that performance might be delayed or might not occur at all, an enforcement provision may make sense. If, however, there is little if any real concern about delay or non-performance, you might consider not bothering with an enforcement provision. Again, address this question to your lawyer. If you are spending too much time worrying about what to do if the other negotiator does not perform the agreement, there might not be enough trust necessary to do the deal with this particular negotiator. If your BATNA is really good, do the deal with someone else!

- *Draft the Agreement.* The negotiators should decide who drafts the final agreement. If the agreement is simple and straightforward, one of the negotiators can draft it at the table, the other can review it and propose revisions, and the final version can be signed by both parties that day.

Some businesses use standard form contracts for certain types of routine transactions. Other times, the terms and conditions of the agreement may be complex, and the written agreement may need to be drafted after the negotiation ends. The negotiator who accepts the task of writing the agreement has the power to choose the language, subject to the other negotiator's power to insist on revisions. For this reason, in most states, the law will interpret the language of the agreement strictly against the party who drafts it and in favor of the party who did not. Again, any questions about how the agreement should be drafted should be addressed to your attorney. If an agreement must contain legal language to create enforceable rights and responsibilities, it may be best to have it drafted by an attorney.

Reaching an agreement at the conclusion of a negotiation is where strategic negotiators shine. They know that they must be precise and clear, making sure that both parties know and understand the terms and conditions of the agreement. Successful negotiators also promptly follow through on getting the written agreement drafted and signed. Delay only provides an opportunity for the deal to be reconsidered or renegotiated. The strategic negotiator understands that closing the deal is all about the details.

In the CD-ROM accompanying this book, you will find a Closing Checklist for your use and reference as you prepare for and conclude any negotiation. There is no single checklist for every negotiation, and each deal is unique, but the Closing Checklist covers most subjects that need to be addressed when closing any deal.

We have almost completed our exploration of strategic negotiating. Our discussion would be incomplete, however, if we did not address ethical issues and common problems that can arise in negotiations. Closing a great deal may create more problems than it solves if you have breached an ethical or legal boundary. There are many common problems that can prevent you from closing the deal at all. These subjects are discussed in the next two chapters.

Key Points to Remember: Chapter 5

1. Preparation is where strategic negotiators shine.
    - Determine your objective.
    - Know your market.
    - Determine your bottom line.
        - BATNA = Best Alternative To a Negotiated Agreement.
        - WATNA = Worst Alternative To a Negotiated Agreement.
        - MLATNA = Most Likely Alternative To a Negotiated Agreement.
        - Be realistic and objective.
        - Avoid overly optimistic BATNA and WATNA.
    - Know your negotiating partner.
    - Anticipate the other negotiator's needs and interests.
    - Plan your opening and responding offer strategy.
    - Determine whether you will negotiate cooperatively, competitively, or both.
2. Make the opening offer to manage the other negotiator's expectations.
3. Let the other negotiator make the opening offer where uncertainty is great.
4. Know when to walk away.
5. When it is time, close the deal.
    - Use time deadlines to motivate decision making.
    - Use anchoring to encourage risk avoidance.
    - Use linkage to find and connect other pies of value to the deal.
    - Brainstorm as a means of creative problem-solving.
    - Hold back important concessions as the last step to close the deal.
    - Establish rapport and use logical persuasion.
    - Use the soft sell to let them come to you.
    - Use the power of walking away if you have leverage.
    - Make the other negotiator feel like the winner.
6. Close the deal when you are satisfied the agreement is durable.
7. Confirm the agreement: be clear and precise about the terms and conditions.
8. Whenever possible, put the agreement in writing.
9. Be flexible and creative about how to close the deal.
10. Re-evaluate your game plan if it is not working.

CHAPTER 6

Ethics in Negotiation

To Be or Not to Be?

M uch has been written on the subject of negotiation ethics. That is because there is no single
guiding set of rules about what is or is not ethical
behavior in a negotiation. What is one negotiator's
appropriate tactic is another's unethical trick. The
word "ethics" has been defined as "a system of moral
principles," or a "branch of philosophy dealing with
values relating to human conduct, with respect to
the rightness and wrongness of certain actions and
to the goodness and badness of the motives and ends
of such actions" (*Random House Compact Unabridged
Dictionary*, 1996). These definitions, however, beg

the question: What do we mean when we use the term "ethics" in relation to negotiation? At best, the concept of negotiation ethics cannot help but be flexible and uncertain, depending upon one's philosophical, moral, cultural, and social context.

Therefore, we will discuss the subject of negotiation ethics from the point of view of generally accepted moral principles, legal standards, and commercial practices in this country. Some guidance does exist for the negotiator about what is and is not ethical behavior in many commonly encountered negotiating situations. In some instances, however, the boundaries are less clear, and much is left to the individual moral values and judgment of the negotiator. Moreover, there is a cultural dimension to the question of negotiation ethics that makes defining a set of clear guidelines difficult; what may seem to us to be ethical conduct in a negotiation may seem the opposite to someone from another culture, and vice versa. Thus, any discussion of negotiation ethics must take into account the possibility that the negotiators come from differing cultural contexts which affect their perceptions of what is and is not ethical behavior in the negotiation.

In order to create guidelines for ethically negotiating, it is helpful to examine the boundaries of acceptable, questionable, and unacceptable negotiator behaviors.

Bluffing, Puffing, and Deception

Regardless of what we *think* we should do as negotiators, what do we *actually do* in negotiations? Are we always completely and totally open and honest with the other negotiator? Before you answer these questions, think of the real world for a moment.

Suppose you are the seller of the classic car in Chapter 1. When the interested prospective buyer approaches you before you write the price on the "For Sale" sign and asks you how much you want for the car, remember the advice we gave you? If maximizing the money you make on the sale is of importance (and it nearly always is or should be), you will balance giving the prospective buyer a price greater than the $6,000 you were getting ready to write on the sign against the possibility he will not negotiate with you and you cannot find another ready and willing buyer. If you were completely and totally open and honest with the prospective buyer, you would lose that choice and say, "I was getting ready to write $6,000 on the sign here." If the prospective buyer said, "Okay, I'll take it right now at that price," what would you think? "I left money on the table, I could have made more." And you would be right. Complete honesty hurt you in this instance.

> ### Negotiating Tip
> Strategic negotiators withhold certain information to their advantage. If the other negotiator knew that you would take a certain price, then an opening offer to sell it at a higher price would not be credible or effective.

So a certain amount of deception often is considered appropriate in negotiations, is it not? Strategic negotiators withhold certain information to their advantage. If the other negotiator knew that you would take a certain price, then an opening offer to sell it at a higher price would not be credible or effective. What expectations would there be to manage if you revealed your bottom line all the time? A person using a cooperative negotiating approach and who is completely honest about his bottom line could be exploited ruthlessly by a competitive negotiator. Not telling the other negotiator what you know or think is an accepted convention in negotiating. Some deception is okay.

In competitive negotiating, bluffing is acceptable as well. This is the practice of making the other negotiator think you have more power or options than you do. For example, if the prospective car buyer approaches you before you put the price on the sign, and indicates the same interest, you might say, "Well, the car is just going on the market, it's a popular model in great condition, I think it's going be in demand, and already there has been a lot of interest in it." You do not have any offers, but you are suggesting that other offers are about to be forthcoming, and people have expressed interest in the car. Bluffing is done to generate further interest and urgency in the prospective buyer that will cause him to pay more than might otherwise be the case. Even though it is deceptive, bluffing is an accepted part of competitively negotiating. Commercial sellers of products bluff all the time when they advertise, "Hurry while supplies last." It may be that the reason there is an advertised sale on the product is that no one has been buying it, so the urgency is not realistic; it is feigned to encourage interest by potential buy-

> **Definition**
>
> Bluffing is the practice of making the other negotiator think you have more power or options than you do.

ers. Bluffing is an accepted part of commercial negotia-tions. Everyone understands and expects it as part of the negotiation dance.

There is another type of bluffing that is more ques-tionable ethically. What if, when the prospective car buyer indicates his interest, you said, "You're just in time. I've had several people approach me to see if I would sell the car, and I have had one offer for $10,000." If this is true, no problem, it is not a bluff. If it is not true that other prospective buyers have expressed interest, or that any of them has offered $10,000 for the car, then the ethical propriety of the statement is ques-tionable. Some say this kind of bluffing is like poker; you pretend you have a better hand than you do. Is this not what we expect when we are bidding on a house or a car? In competitive bargaining, we expect and accept a certain amount of untruthful bluffing.

Yet some rightly would say that intentionally and falsely representing that you have received an offer for a specific amount is unethical. Why do we accept some deceptive bluffing as okay, but other similar behavior as unacceptable? This is a difficult question to answer, but we must try to do better than "I know it when I see it." In the two examples above, the first type of bluffing involved the seller's expression of an opinion about the demand for the car. He has not made a statement of fact, but he has offered an opinion that there will be other offers soon. We accept potentially inac-curate opinions as part of the competitive bargaining process. The manage-ment of expectations by the sending of signals involves a certain degree of deception that the two negotiators, if they are behaving strategically, under-stand and expect.

The second example of bluffing, however, involves the intentionally false statement of fact that an offer at a specific amount has been made. If the cul-ture in which the negotiation occurs accepts this type of falsehood as an appro-priate part of the negotiating ritual, there is no problem. If both negotiators

expect and accept this as normal in such a negotiation, the deception is ritual-
istic and ineffectual; it is a customary part of the process that has no reasonable likelihood of misleading either negotiator. If, however, such falsehoods
are not so accepted in the negotiating culture, then an ethical boundary has
been crossed. And this is the beginning of our understanding of ethical guidelines in negotiating: Whatever behaviors are tolerated, intentionally false and
misleading statements that are designed to induce the other negotiator to rely
on them are fraudulent and unacceptable in the United States and most cultures throughout the world. After all, negotiators expect to obtain truthful
information either directly or indirectly from each other during the negotiation in order to close the deal. Lying about material information necessary to
the durability of the deal is detrimental to the negotiation process and undermines commerce.

For example, what would the commercial world be like if an airline company is told by the seller that a hydraulic system upon which the jet's steering
depends is of a certain quality and construction, when in fact it is not? If the
difference is a negligent mistake, there will be legal liability requiring compensation. If the seller has purpose-
fully misrepresented the quality and construction of the
hydraulic system, then the airline company can sue the
seller for fraud and recover any losses it suffered plus
punitive damages. Fraud—the intentional misrepresenta-
tion of a material fact that harms another—is illegal and
unethical. This ethical boundary line is clear.

Even if it were not illegal and unethical, intentional
falsehood is also detrimental to any hope of cooperative
bargaining. A lie might be something we expect in a car
deal, to some extent. The dealer might say that his cost
for a car is X, when it is really Y, a lower number. The
buyer might say another dealer can sell the car to him for Y, when the best
offer he has is a little less than X. While we view dishonesty in any form as
morally and professionally unsound, these kinds of misrepresentations are
common in commercial deals and most people expect them. In most

> **Negotiating Tip**
>
> Intentionally false and mis-
> leading statements of fact
> that are designed to induce
> the other negotiator to rely
> on them are fraudulent and
> unacceptable. Lying about
> material information is
> detrimental to the
> negotiation process.

competitive negotiating, future interaction and ongoing cooperation after the deal is not valued or realistic.

In cooperative negotiating, however, typically there is an ongoing business or personal relationship that is being built or served. Lying is the quickest way to destroy the trust necessary to create a durable agreement through cooperative negotiating. It is also fatal to ongoing relationships, and it creates conflict in future interactions. So not only is lying about material facts an unethical negotiating practice in many cultures, it is counter-productive in most instances, particularly where cooperative negotiating is necessary to create durable agreements.

For example, consider this fictional story of a brother and sister and their mother's estate. The brother, whom we will call Joshua, cared for his elderly mother in the last several years of her life. His sister, Rebecca, lived in another state, but she visited her mother and brother several times each year. Many years before the mother became ill and needed care, she had executed a written will leaving all of her belongings, including some money and the family home, to both Joshua and Rebecca in equal shares. Joshua and Rebecca were never close, but they got along reasonably well, and Rebecca was grateful that Joshua cared for their mother in the years leading to her death.

Prior to the mother's death, Joshua and Rebecca had several conversations about the estate. Joshua assured Rebecca that the family home had no mortgage, and that there had been no changes in the will. After the mother died, however, Rebecca learned that Joshua had taken a large mortgage out on the house in order to finance his small printing business. There was no suggestion that Joshua was unable or unwilling to repay the loan, as his business was thriving and he signed a promissory note for the entire amount of the mortgage. But Rebecca was hurt and felt betrayed by Joshua's apparent dishonesty. He had told her the house was owned free and clear, and he had secretly mortgaged it. The distrust this created had a strong negative effect on Joshua and Rebecca's relationship. At a time in their lives when they should have been getting closer, they grew farther apart. Dishonesty, particularly concerning money, can have that effect on business and personal relationships. Therefore, even if a certain amount of deception would be acceptable in competitive negotiating, it can be terribly destructive in cooperative negotiating, in which trust and relationships are important components of any deal.

Finally, there is the deception of puffing. Puffing is the act of overstating the quality or benefits of the good or service being negotiated. "It is the number one cell phone on the market!" "No one beats our prices—no one!" "Drive home in the best compact car on the market." These statements are boasts, expressions of opinion, about the quality or benefits of the services or products being negotiated. In virtually every culture, such hyperbole is expected and accepted as a part of commercial life. They are also accepted as universally untrustworthy. Thus, in this instance, a common deception in negotiating is ethically acceptable because everyone knows the rules and no one is misled. And that is the best way of determining whether a practice in negotiating is ethical or not: 1) Do both negotiators understand and expect it; and 2) Does it have any tendency to mislead either negotiator?

> **Negotiating Tip**
>
> It is unethical to state as fact something you know is false, but bluffing and puffing are an accepted and expected feature of competitive negotiating.

In the business world, you earn your reputation by what you say and do. Regardless of whether deception on some order is commonplace in a type of transaction, avoiding intentionally false statements of fact is the preferred practice. Lying simply is not good business.

Honesty in Negotiating

"Honesty is the best policy." This is a fundamental moral and ethical value in most cultures. But, as mentioned in the previous section, complete honesty, that is, sharing all the information you have with the other negotiator, is a recipe for being exploited. Permitting the other negotiator to take advantage of you is not a moral or ethical value in most cultures. So while honesty is high on the list of fundamental moral and ethical values that should guide negotiators, it must be managed in a strategic way that helps and does not hinder the negotiator's objectives.

One way of being strategically honest in a negotiation is to truthfully answer questions when doing so will not harm your cause. For example, if you are the car seller in Chapter 1, the prospective buyer might ask you, "How long has it been for sale?" You could truthfully answer, "Today is the first day on the market." This does not undermine your objective of getting the best price. The other negotiator does get information useful to him or her—that there have not likely been any offers on it yet—but that is unavoidable. Negotiations involve the reciprocal exchange of information when it is useful to both negotiators to advance the negotiating process. In order for the information to have value to the recipient, it must be truthful.

Another way to be strategically honest is to not answer a question when it serves your best interest to do so and does not undermine the negotiation. For example, if the prospective car buyer asks, "Will you give me a good deal if I buy it from you now?" you might not answer that question. Instead, you might say, "I'm selling it for $8,000." You have not been dishonest: you were planning on selling it for $6,000, but an eager buyer has encouraged you to ask for more. You have not, however, answered his question. A competitive negotiator in the prospective buyer's position will understand why you did not answer the question; it was asking for more information than you should reveal. Not answering a question can be an effective means of avoiding a lie or revealing truthful information that is harmful to you.

There are times, however, when you cannot avoid answering a question honestly. For example, when you are selling a home, most states require that you make certain disclosures concerning the home's condition, including prior water leaks, land subsidence, and the like. These conditions are usually deemed to be material to the buyer's decision to purchase the property. The seller does not have the option to avoid answering these questions under state law; not providing the necessary information or providing untruthful information exposes the seller to liability for fraudulent nondisclosure. There are many other situations in which a truthful answer must be given to a negotiator's question in order to avoid committing fraud: the mileage on a car in an automobile sale, the age of a horse in a negotiation for the purchase of the animal, the receipts and expenses of a business in a negotiation for the purchase the business, prior work experience in an employment negotiation, hardware and software included in a computer purchase, and the list goes on. These are just a few of the many instances in which information must be truthfully provided by law. Thus, in many transactions, honesty is the best policy to help businesses comply with state and federal laws.

Finally, whether it is ethically or legally required, honesty can have a commercial value. We have heard the expression, "One does well by doing good." Happy customers and clients help businesses grow, and unhappy customers and clients do the opposite. Perhaps a company that is the only game in town and sells a product in high demand can afford to be dishonest in its negotiations with its customers, but most businesses in a competitive market cannot. Good will is an important asset of any business, and nothing minimizes its value more than a reputation for dishonest negotiating. Reputations, good and bad, are built over time and they can be destroyed in the blink of an eye by dishonesty. So honesty may be viewed not simply as an ethical or moral question, but as an economic one as well. Honesty can be the most important asset a business possesses.

> **Negotiating Tip**
>
> Honesty is the best policy, but be strategic about answering questions, and always make disclosures as required by law.

Cultural and Moral Norms

What is and is not expected and appropriate in a negotiation depends upon the negotiators' perspectives. When both negotiators come from the same culture, or share the same moral values, they both understand their negotiating process. For example, it may be normal in a culture for the negotiators to demonstrate what is referred to as "ritual opposition," that is, it is customary for negotiators in that culture to resist agreement and to demonstrate opposition as part of the negotiating dance. For example, a buyer at a farmer's market in Latin America might engage in spirited disagreement with the seller, including the waving of hands and frequent protestations of inability to reach a deal. The word "no" might be uttered frequently throughout the extended discussions. And yet, they reach agreement on a price, and they both end the negotiation happy. Both negotiators understand and accept this behavior as part of the negotiating process, even though it is not strictly honest. It is play acting. Neither negotiator is misled, the behavior is expected and accepted, and the process works for both negotiators. This negotiation ritual is their dance.

Cultural and moral values cause problems in negotiations, however, when both negotiators are not on the same page. For example, one negotiator may be from a culture that favors honesty and disfavors ritual opposition in negotiating, while the other negotiator comes from a culture that expects and accepts a great degree of deception and ritual opposition in negotiating. This dynamic frequently results in conflict during negotiations. An American negotiator for a video distributor, for instance, might perceive that the Italian negotiator for a video rental chain is being dishonest and uncooperative by refusing to disclose rental volume figures and repeatedly saying, "That's impossible," during their negotiation. The American negotiator might pass up a lucrative sale because he does not understand and adapt to the Italian negotiator's use of ritual opposition in the negotiation. With the increasing pace of cultural diversity, mismatches of expectations and perceptions in the negotiating process are a daily challenge to reaching durable agreements. When negotiators are not on the same page concerning proper negotiating behavior, misunderstanding and conflict can be impediments to reaching deals.

> **Negotiating Tip**
>
> Cultural and moral values cause problems in negotiations when negotiators are not on the same page. Misunderstanding and conflict can be impediments to reaching deals.

There are several steps the strategic negotiator takes to avoid the pitfalls of cross-cultural mismatch of expectations about negotiation ethics:

- Obtain reliable information about the culture of the other negotiator through research before employing negotiation or questioning techniques during the negotiation.
- Avoid stereotypes and misconceptions about that culture.
- Do not automatically attribute deception and opposition to dishonesty or bad moral values.
- Educate the other negotiator about your expectations concerning honesty and opposition in the negotiation.

- Work with a consultant and translator who can advise you about any cultural issues that may affect the negotiation.

In addition, remember the three steps of cooperative negotiating:

1. Be soft on the people, hard on the issue;
2. Go below the line to discover the other negotiator's underlying interests; and
3. Explore options with the potential for mutual gain.

Patience, listening, and questioning are effective techniques for strategically managing mismatched expectations regarding appropriate negotiating behavior. Reacting angrily or impatiently to what you perceive to be negative or unethical negotiating behaviors exhibited by someone from another culture is not strategic and can kill deals.

Here is a final anecdote that demonstrates how two business negotiators from different cultures can completely miss out on negotiating a mutually profitable deal. During a visit to China, one of the authors witnessed the following failed negotiation while checking his e-mail at the business center of a hotel. There he saw a German man engaged in discussions with three Chinese men. They were using English as their negotiating language, but none of them spoke it well. From what could be overheard, the German negotiator represented a large European distributor of toys, and the Chinese negotiators represented the owners of a Chinese manufacturer of toys and other consumer goods. The German negotiator told the Chinese negotiators that his company was interested in placing a "sizable" order, "something in the range of $2 million U.S. dollars." The Chinese negotiators appeared eager to please.

The German negotiator asked for a brochure or some printed material concerning the types of products the Chinese manufacturer had produced in a volume similar to that contemplated by the European company. The Chinese negotiators had no idea what the German negotiator was saying. The German negotiator tried inexpertly to explain what he meant, but his English was not good and he started to use German words more familiar to him. The Chinese negotiators' English was much less accomplished than that of the

German negotiator and their German was non-existent. The German negotiator and his Chinese counterparts went on like this for half an hour, like two ships passing slowly and painfully in the night. Finally, the German negotiator gave up and left his bewildered Chinese counterparts at the table wondering what had happened. These negotiators could have reached a deal if they spoke the same language and understood their respective expectations. Without a common language and understanding, they could not reach a deal.

In an increasingly interdependent and diverse negotiating world, culture, perception, and language play a greater role in negotiators either understanding or misunderstanding each other. The strategic negotiator gathers the information necessary to attempt to overcome these barriers. Good negotiators also understand that negotiation ethics may differ depending on culture. This wisdom is particularly valuable in the business world: To grow and profit in an increasingly global economy, you must understand and successfully work with negotiators of different cultures to reach deals. In order to drive to your destination, you have to be able to read the map.

Legal Limits on Negotiating Behavior and Agreements

The law places limits on agreements in a variety of situations. We do not attempt to discuss the many different ways in which state and federal laws might affect negotiating behavior and the agreements reached in negotiations. That effort would involve a book much larger and more technical than this one. Instead, we provide an overview of the types of legal limitations throughout the United States that affect negotiating behavior and the kinds of agreements negotiations produce. As always, consult a licensed and experienced attorney concerning the legal implications of any business or negotiation decision.

Duty to Disclose

As mentioned previously, the law may impose a duty on a negotiator to disclose truthful information to the other negotiator before a deal is reached. The most common examples are the duties imposed on sellers of real estate to disclose the condition of the property, and the duties on automobile dealers to disclose accurate information concerning the condition of the cars they sell, including mileage, whether the vehicle is new or used, and any prior accidents in which the car was involved. State and federal consumer protection laws extend such duties to other sellers of products and services as well.

Additionally, if one negotiator is in a trust or fiduciary relationship with the other negotiator, the former owes a duty of disclosing material facts to the latter. Examples of such trust or fiduciary relationships include lawyers and

> **Definition**
>
> Duty to disclose is the duty on a negotiator to disclose truthful information to the other negotiator before a deal is reached.

their clients, agents and their principals, officers and directors to their shareholders, business partners to each other, trustees and beneficiaries, and spouses toward each other in many states. Dishonesty or deception in a negotiation between one who has a fiduciary duty toward another can give rise to an action to set aside the agreement for actual or constructive fraud. Also, one who has fiduciary duties must avoid what the law refers to as self-dealing, that is, negotiating a deal that is great for him but against the best interests of the person to whom the negotiator owes a duty of trust.

Fraud

It is illegal for one negotiator to make a false statement of material fact with the intent to induce the other negotiator to enter into an agreement, which false statement induces the other negotiator to enter into the agreement, and that ultimately causes harm or damage to the other negotiator (e.g., loss of money). Any such conduct is called fraud. For example, suppose you are negotiating a home loan from a bank. You tell the bank you make more money and have more assets than you do so that the bank will loan you enough money to buy the house you want, or so you can get that business loan. The bank believes you and loans you the money. You have committed fraud on the bank; the bank would not have loaned you the amount of money it did had you disclosed your true income and assets.

Another type of fraud happens when you have a legal duty to disclose information to the other negotiator, but you either negligently or intentionally fail to do so (such as in the case mentioned earlier of one negotiator having a trust or fiduciary relationship with the other). This is called fraudulent non-disclosure.

Unfair Business Practices

Many states, including California, have laws prohibiting what are referred to as "unfair or deceptive business practices" (see California Business and Professions Code, Sections 17200, et seq.). If a business uses deceptive advertising, such as listing a product for sale at a certain price but charging the customer more money for the same thing, that is an unfair or deceptive business practice. Using any form of deception or dishonesty in consumer negotiations may expose the business to civil or criminal penalties under these laws. In some instances, a business may be subject to criminal investigation and prosecution by a state attorney general or the local prosecutor for using any unfair or deceptive practice in a negotiation. An example of such prohibited conduct in a negotiation may include saying you have a product in your inventory when you do not, saying that your cost for an item is different than it is, or making an offer to perform a service or deliver a product when you have no ability to honor the offer.

> **Definition**
>
> A business that uses deceptive advertising, such as listing a product for sale at a certain price but charging the customer more money for the same thing, is using an unfair or deceptive business practice.

If you are in business, check with your state and local consumer protection agencies for information on how to avoid engaging in an unfair or deceptive business practice. Conform your negotiations to the law. If you have any doubt about whether the way your business negotiates with consumers may be an unfair or deceptive business practice, consult with a licensed and experienced attorney. Play it safe!

Undue Influence, Duress, and Coercion

In certain instances, an agreement may be void and unenforceable if it is created as the result of what is called undue influence, duress, or coercion. Simply stated, anything a negotiator does to undermine the other negotiator's exercise of free will in entering an agreement can be legally challenged in most states as undue influence, coercion, or duress depending on the conduct involved. The situations in which this may occur vary. Undue influence is more likely to be found when a business, caregiver, or trustee seeks to enforce an agreement with an elderly person, a child, or a dependent adult. Where a person is susceptible to undue influence, duress, or coercion, the law is more likely to find that has occurred if the agreement is too one-sided or unfair.

> **Definition**
>
> Anything a negotiator does to undermine the other negotiator's exercise of free will in entering an agreement can be challenged as undue influence, coercion, or duress.

For example, undue influence frequently is found to have occurred when a door-to-door salesperson uses aggressive tactics to get an elderly person to buy a product. Coercion or duress may have occurred when a customer is prevented from leaving an automobile dealership after an hours-long negotiation. A contract that is signed by a tired, unsophisticated negotiator at 2:00 A.M. after 12 hours of tough negotiating may be the product of coercion or undue influence. Negotiators should avoid any kind of strong-arm tactics that override the other negotiator's free will, particularly when the other negotiator is not sophisticated or is particularly vulnerable.

Illegal Contracts

Any agreement that violates the law or the public policies expressed by the law is treated in most states as either void or voidable. A void contract is unenforceable. A voidable contract may be broken within a certain period of time at the option of the aggrieved party. For example, some states prohibit contracts that require a negotiator to waive important legal protections, such as notice and redemption rights in nonjudicial foreclosures of real property mortgages. Those states treat such waivers as void and unenforceable even though the negotiators agreed upon them. Of course, any agreement to commit a crime is also void and unenforceable. Contracts with minors or incompetent adults are also void in most states.

Contracts Requiring Court Approval

In many states, agreements involving minors, divorcing spouses, and incompetent adults must receive court approval to be enforceable. For example, in some states, a property division agreement between divorcing spouses must be approved by the court in order to be enforceable. Without such approval, the agreement is void, even though the spouses negotiated it freely, voluntarily, and with the advice of legal counsel. In many states, contracts negotiated by guardians or conservators of elderly or dependent adults are subject to court review and approval at some point, either before they are entered into or afterward.

These are just a sample of limitations the law places on negotiations and agreements. The effective negotiator must know the legal limits and implications of the agreements she negotiates. If you have any questions concerning the legal limits and implications of any agreement you are negotiating, or if you think you might be involved in any of the situations described above, consult with a licensed and knowledgeable attorney. It is better to be safe than sorry.

Ultimately, your negotiation ethics are up to you. Balancing strategy with ethics is the hallmark of the best negotiators. Deals come and go, but reputations—good and bad—last a lifetime.

> **Negotiating Tip**
>
> Ultimately, your negotiation ethics are up to you. Balancing strategy with ethics is the hallmark of the best negotiators. Deals come and go, but reputations—good and bad—last a lifetime.

Key Points to Remember: Chapter 6

1. Negotiating ethics begin with your personal, moral, and business values.

2. Bluffing (pretending you have more leverage or options than you do) is okay.

3. Puffing (extolling the virtues of your product or services) is also okay—to an extent.

4. Lying (intentionally misstating a material fact) is not okay and is probably fraudulent.

5. Honesty is the best policy, but be strategic about it.

6. Be careful to know the legal limits and implications of agreements you negotiate.

7. Where there is a duty to disclose information truthfully, just do it!

8. Take extra care when negotiating in matters involving the elderly and minors.

9. Be culturally literate: both negotiators should understand the rules of the dance.

10. When in doubt about the legality of a negotiating behavior or agreement, consult an attorney.

CHAPTER 7

Common Problems in Negotiating

and Recommended Solutions

The effective strategic negotiator should be ready for anything in every negotiation. In this section, we identify some of the most common problems that arise in negotiations, and we make some recommendations about how to deal with them.

Impediments to Decision Making

Frequently, the ability of the negotiators to make decisions necessary to agreement is impaired. Here are a few of the most common impediments to decision making during a negotiation and some recommended ways of overcoming them.

Absent Decision Maker and Lack of Authority

Sometimes, an important decision maker is not directly engaged in the negotiation. This can happen in different ways. For example, a decision maker may send a subordinate or agent to the negotiation on her behalf. During the negotiation, it becomes clear that an important element to reaching final agreement is missing—the consent of the absent decision maker. This can be inadvertent; sometimes, it is unavoidable. For example, the company cannot afford to send a senior manager to the negotiation, so a junior employee attends instead. Other times, it is an intentional tactic and the negotiating team is strategically imposing a two-step negotiating process that makes it harder to extract concessions from them. Common examples of this situation are when you are negotiating with an insurance adjuster who answers to a claims manager who is not present, or in negotiating with a sales representative who answers to a district sales manager at the home office.

The authors have experienced this situation many times, and one incident stands out. One of us served as a mediator in a major lawsuit. A mediation is a type of negotiation in which a neutral third person—the mediator—assists the parties in negotiating. Before the mediation, the mediator's standard procedure was to call the lawyers representing the parties to gather any information that may be important to preparing for the mediation. In the course of doing so, one of the authors spoke with the lawyer representing the defendant. When asked who would be at the mediation, the lawyer said, "Beth Johnson, the adjuster handling the file." The mediator asked, "Does she have all the authority she needs to make any and all decisions necessary during the mediation?" The lawyer answered matter-of-factly, "Oh, no. That person is her manager, and he is in New Jersey. He won't be there." The mediator paused. "Have you mentioned this to the plaintiff's lawyer?" The defense lawyer responded, "No." The mediator then asked, "Why not?" The defense attorney laughed, "I don't think he'd attend the mediation if I told him that!"

The reason the defense attorney did not want to tell the plaintiff's attorney about the absent decision maker is because the plaintiff's attorney would likely tell him, "No decision maker, no negotiation." The absent decision maker is commonly used as a tactic to make it harder to offer concessions in a negotiation, or of changing a deal later. Here are some ways of handling this situation.

Recommended Solution

Anticipate the problem and negotiate the process. Prior to the negotiation, find out who is going to be negotiating and whether he has all the authority he needs to finalize a deal. Ask whether any other consents or approvals are necessary, and if so, insist that those people will be present. If the other negotiating team wishes to use the two-step process, indicate that you may do likewise, which could lengthen the negotiations. If time is of the essence, propose that the decision makers negotiate in person or by telephone directly. Another alternative is to insist that the negotiator present be granted complete authority to negotiate, as opposed to having to get permission from the absent decision maker.

> **Negotiating Tip**
>
> When an absent decision maker is used as an intentional tactic by a negotiating team, they are strategically imposing a two-step negotiating process that makes it harder to extract concessions from them.

In some instances, you might not be able to avoid absent decision makers. Corporations and governmental entities frequently negotiate through surrogates who need to have their deals approved by a governing body. Unions and management negotiate through teams of representatives whose deals must be approved by their respective principals. When decision makers are absent unavoidably, get the assurance of the negotiator that she has authority to negotiate and that she will recommend the agreement to the ultimate decision maker. If the other negotiating team reneges on the tentative agreement or wishes to renegotiate terms later, you may need to withdraw concessions you have made in order to avoid being exploited.

In the above story, the mediator told the defense attorney, "Well, you need to tell plaintiff's counsel. If it is okay with her, it's okay with me, provided the claims manager is available by telephone, including after business hours." The mediator negotiated process with the defense attorney, and insisted the defense attorney do so with the plaintiff's attorney. That way, all parties were on the same page about how to engage all decision makers in the negotiation, and the effects of a negative tactic were avoided or minimized.

Lack of Information

A negotiation may stall if either or both of the negotiators lack information necessary to evaluate the proposed deal in comparison to their respective BATNA (Best Alternative to Negotiated Agreement), WATNA (Worst Alternative to Negotiated Agreement), and MLATNA (Most Likely Alternative to Negotiated Agreement). In other instances, the quality of a product, good, or property must be determined reliably in order for the deal to be reached. For example, in baseball or football contract negotiations, the player must pass a medical examination as an important precondition to agreement. Sometimes, the information for an appraisal of a business or of real property must be gathered before the agreement can be reached. A bank cannot fulfill its loan agreement without an appraisal of the fair market value of the home that is securing the loan.

One of the authors serves as the mediator of disputes between family members involving wills, trusts, and estates. In one such dispute, a brother and a sister were negotiating who should get what share of their father's estate. The only asset in the estate was the father's run-down house. The brother thought the house was worth $600,000. The sister thought the house was worth $350,000. They could not effectively negotiate their respective shares of the house without knowing how much they were conceding, so they agreed to have an appraiser provide an opinion about the house's fair market value in its current dilapidated condition. The appraised fair market value of the home was $425,000. With that information, the brother and sister were able to successfully negotiate an agreement dividing their interests.

When information is a stumbling block to making decisions in the negotiation, there is a simple approach to follow.

Recommended Solution

Negotiate a process for obtaining the necessary information within a specific time. Ideally, you should not need to delay the negotiation to find out your BATNA, WATNA, and MLATNA. You should have obtained reliable information about your options before the negotiation. If there is no risk, you will fail to get what you need, you can stop negotiating while you determine your BATNA, WATNA and MLATNA by investigating the market and talking with other potential negotiating partners. Where information is necessary to establish the value being negotiated, agree with the other negotiator on a process to obtain the information as soon as possible. Set clear time guidelines for obtaining the information.

Avoid using the desire for more information as an excuse to delay negotiating or decision making, as this can kill the deal or result in worse terms later. Sometimes delaying the negotiation to get more information is simply a tactic to improve a negotiator's bargaining position or put off making a decision. Consider this fictional story of two brothers negotiating the reorganization of their successful family farm. The two brothers, Delbert and Abe, had worked the farm for over 30 years. It had seen some hard times, but, with the help of modern technology and savvy planning, the farm had prospered by providing organic specialty produce to restaurants and farmer's markets. It was time for the two brothers to pass the reins to someone else in the family, but who? Delbert's son-in-law, Woodrow, was Delbert's choice. Abe, however, felt Woodrow needed some seasoning.

The two brothers hired experts and consultants to help them structure a plan for when it was time to retire. Every time Delbert and Abe sat down to sign the paperwork on the reorganization plan, however, Abe needed more information. "Do we have the projections for seasonal herbs five years down the road?" Or, "What about pears? We've got a good climate and soil for them, and they're very profitable. Maybe we should get some projections on pears before we decide how to structure things." Delbert became increasingly frustrated with Abe's need for more information. Finally, the fifth or sixth time Abe asked to delay the signing of documents because he wanted more information, Delbert asked him angrily, "Abe. What the hell's the matter? You keep putting this off. Just tell it to me straight." Abe admitted that he did not think Woodrow had the right stuff to run the farm, and

> **Negotiating Tip**
>
> Sometimes delaying the negotiation to get more information is simply a tactic to improve a negotiator's bargaining position or put off making a decision.

he refused to sign paperwork that handed over control to him. Delbert's feelings were hurt, but he understood, and he revealed to Abe that he shared some of the same concerns. Eventually, the two brothers came to an agreement in which Woodrow would be mentored by Delbert and Abe until he was ready. Abe was delaying an agreement by requesting more information because he did not know how to tell Delbert about his lack of confidence in Woodrow.

The moral of this story is that the strategic negotiator always knows whether additional information is necessary to reach an informed decision, or whether it is simply a way of buying time or putting off a difficult decision. When information is essential to making accurate decisions in the negotiation, get it in the fastest, most reliable way possible.

Another form of information people may need comes from experts, consultants, or attorneys. A technical question about an office network server may be essential to reaching a deal in a negotiation. In that situation, you may want to hire an expert or consultant to determine how to address the technical question. Sometimes, you may need to know the legal limits and ramifications of certain deal points. In those instances, it is best to consult with a licensed and experienced attorney to assist you in gaining the information you need to properly negotiate a deal.

Differing Communication Styles

People send and receive messages by eye contact, body language, vocal tone, and word content. Personality, intellect, culture, life experiences, gender, and language ability are among the many influences on how we communicate. There are so many filters through which communication passes that it's a wonder we can communicate at all! Certainly, all of these challenges exist in negotiating, which is, after all, a process of communication between two or more people trying to reach agreement.

Polychronic and Monochronic Processing Styles

Psychologists, sociologists, and behavioral scientists have identified a nettlesome challenge people encounter when they communicate with each other.

One of our colleagues, Nina Meierding, has summarized this research in the following way. Some people are naturally monochronic, that is, they process information in a linear fashion. These people thrive on order, and they love lists. They also tend to be single-task oriented, and they do not like to be interrupted. For example, a monochronic person who is on the phone is likely to be annoyed to the point of distraction if someone tries to get her attention by waving or passing a note. "I'm on the phone!" would be the monochronic person's desperate plea. The monochronic person would leave this interaction feeling irritated. The person just trying to interject useful information would be irritated by the monochronic person's irritation!

> **Definition**
>
> People who are monochronic process information in a linear fashion. They thrive on order and they love lists. They also tend to be single-task oriented, and they do not like to be interrupted.

Polychronic people can do many things at once, and they do not mind going from one thing to the next. Polychronic people love brainstorming, and they may engage in what is referred to as "overlapping talk," supportive interruptions during conversation that establish agreement, understanding, and rapport with other polychronic people. The polychronic person's list is not likely to be linear, but going out in different directions.

Polychronic and monochronic people frequently conflict in their efforts to communicate. The monochronic person may think that the polychronic person is scattered, interrupts, cannot stay focused, and is maddeningly disorganized. The polychronic person may think that the monochronic person is too rigid, not terribly creative, and difficult to work with. When a polychronic person negotiates with a monochronic person, there is a high likelihood of mutual frustration, disagreement, or misunderstanding. If you see yourself as either monochronic or polychronic, these differing perceptions might seem familiar to you.

> **Definition**
>
> Polychronic people can do many things at once, and don't mind going quickly from one thing to the next. They love brainstorming and engage in what is referred to as "overlapping talk" with other polychronic people.

For example, consider the fictional story of two people, Julie and Diane, who own a travel agency. They have been business partners for years, and the agency has done very well. Recently, however, Julie and Diane began to have conflict about future expansion. Julie, who has handled the financial aspect of the business from the beginning, does not think expansion is a good idea. She wants to invest the business's surplus cash in stocks, bonds, and certificates of deposit to grow a cash reserve. Diane, who is a genius at marketing and client relationships, thinks Julie is being foolishly cautious. Diane believes that the agency must grow so it can compete, and that changes in the travel business dictate expansion sooner rather than later. Their disagreement escalated, so they sought the assistance of a mediator.

It became apparent to the mediator that Julie was monochronic and Diane was polychronic. When they began their travel agency, Diane admired Julie's organization, discipline, and work ethic. Julie seemed to have a head for the financial end of the business. Diane, on the other hand, was a "big picture" person, who loved to create new ideas for growing the business. Julie admired this quality in Diane, because Julie was not very creative, and she hated dealing with people. Their differences were complimentary in this way and the business grew because of their combined strengths. Unfortunately, their communication processing styles were polar opposites, which caused innumerable misunderstandings and conflict.

The strategic negotiator must assess whether misunderstanding, disagreement, or conflict with the other negotiator is the result of a mismatch between polychronic and monochronic communication processing styles. If the problem is the result of these differing communication processing styles, there are ways of strategically responding to the situation to achieve agreement.

Recommended Solution

We cannot change who we are, but there are techniques for improving communication between negotiators with these differing processing styles. First, recognize the problem is one of communication processing style, not necessarily of personality or intellect. Second, adapt your communication to accommodate the other person. A polychronic person is more likely to be successful doing so than the monochronic person, while flexibility comes more easily to the former than the latter. Still, the monochronic person can identify the polychronic processing style and adapt accordingly by being patient, listening effectively, and focusing the conversation at appropriate intervals. Patience, listening, and choosing language that is soft on the people and hard on the issues is a great way to overcome communication processing differences. It is also the key to cooperative negotiating generally.

For example, suppose you are polychronic and your negotiating partner is monochronic. From your point of view, the negotiation is going fine; you are offering many different options for discussion, changing the order as you go. You notice that the other negotiator is silent and seems to be either overwhelmed or upset. If what you know about the other negotiator leads you to suspect that she might have a monochronic processing style, stop for a moment, and ask her, "Is the way we are discussing this working for you?" The other negotiator might say, "I don't understand." You could say, "How would you like to approach this discussion?" to which the other negotiator might respond, "Well, how about if we take these ideas one at a time, develop them, and then

> ### Negotiating Tip
>
> Patience, listening, and choosing language that is soft on people and hard on issues is a great way to overcome communication processing differences.

move on to the next item?" You have invited a change in the process of your negotiation by identifying the problem, diagnosing it as a communication issue, and adjusting your conversation accordingly in a way that works for both negotiators. And that is the bottom line of a successful negotiation: a communication process that works for both negotiators and produces a satisfying and durable agreement.

The monochronic negotiator might respond to a polychronic negotiator similarly. The monochronic negotiator who is getting frustrated and distracted by the volume of differing topics offered by the polychronic negotiator might say, "I'm glad that you've come to our discussion prepared to offer ideas. I want to hear them all. Would it be okay with you if we slowed down a bit, and took each idea one at a time, so I can make sure I understand what you're thinking?" This approach, again, invites a negotiation about the process of the negotiation itself, shaping the communication in a way that works for both negotiators. This approach also avoids the monochronic person's automatic internal response, which is that the polychronic negotiator is "scattered" or "flaky" or "disorganized" or "nutty." These negative reactions invariably cause problems for the monochronic negotiator unless they are strategically managed.

The mediator helped Julie and Diane work out their communication problems in exactly this way. Julie learned to be patient with Diane's "scattered" approach to conversation, while Diane learned to be patient with Julie's "rigid" focus in discussions. With some education about how to manage their differing communication styles, Julie and Diane had a very creative, but focused agenda for their negotiation about expansion. In that process, they came up with a wonderful business plan that has proven to be very successful. More importantly, their working relationship has improved because they have learned to make adjustments in how they communicate with each other. Many problems of communication in business negotiations can be resolved in this way.

Unrealistic Risk/Benefit Assessment

A negotiator may overestimate or underestimate his BATNA, WATNA, or MLATNA. When this happens, the negotiator loses a valuable tool: an objective and reasonable basis upon which to decide whether to take the deal at the table or hold out for a better deal elsewhere.

Your Risk/Benefit Assessment Is Unrealistic

No one is immune to excessive optimism or negativism. It is normal for people to have an unrealistically optimistic view of their BATNA, WATNA, or MLATNA. For example, it is common for negotiators involved in litigation to be convinced that their view of the case will prevail, and that the best possible outcome in court is much better or more probable than it is, and that the worst possible outcome is less bad and less probable than it is. A negotiator who does this is likely to mistake his overly optimistic BATNA for his MLATNA, that is, the negotiator believes that his best *possible* deal away from the table is what will *likely* happen. When this occurs, the negotiator is using tainted information to decide what to do: take the deal or hold out for a better one that might not occur. Worse, unrealistic outcome expectations can mean turning down a good deal and ending up with a bad one. The reverse is also true: your BATNA, WATNA, and MLATNA may be better than you think, and you may negotiate an outcome that is considerably worse than you would likely get away from the table (e.g., in court, or with another negotiating partner).

Recommended Solution

Obtain objective and reliable information about your options away from the negotiating table. You can do this by investigating what other providers of a good or service are offering and for how much. In the context of lawsuits, get your lawyer's opinion about your courtroom BATNA, WATNA, and MLATNA, along with the bases

> ### Negotiating Tip
>
> When a negotiator over- or underestimates her BATNA, WATNA, or MLATNA, she loses a valuable tool: the objective and reasonable basis upon which to decide whether to take the deal at the table or hold out for a better one.

of her opinion in that regard. Ask your lawyer about jury verdicts and judgments in similar cases. "Have you ever tried any cases like this one?" If the answer is "yes," then ask, "How did they turn out?" If there is a lot of information about how lawsuits like yours are resolved in court in your jurisdiction, an opinion about your BATNA, WATNA, and MLATNA is based on solid information, and is likely to be more reliable. If there is little or no such information, any opinion about your BATNA, WATNA, and MLATNA is less reliable, and the courtroom holds much more risk for you. In that environment, minimize your BATNA, maximize your WATNA, and view your MLATNA with skepticism—it is speculative at best.

Businesses need to take extra care in assessing their BATNAs, WATNAs and MLATNAs. This is done through careful analysis—gather reliable and objective information, and make projections based upon reasonable and conservative assumptions. For example, responsible financial planning dictates that budgets are created based upon conservative estimates of revenue and liberal estimates of operating expenses. The key for any budget projection is to be pleasantly surprised. Ideally, actual revenue is greater and actual expenses are less than forecast. The reverse experience—actual revenue is less and actual expenses are greater than estimated—is an unpleasant surprise that most businesses try to avoid. The same approach is true for estimating your BATNA, WATNA, and MLATNA. Assume that your best possible outcome away from the table is not as good as it might be, that your worst outcome is worse than it might be, and your most probable outcome is less good than it likely is. If you use this approach, you minimize the likelihood of unrealistically assessing your options away from the negotiating table.

The Other Negotiator's Risk/Benefit Assessment Is Unrealistic

Remember that the effective negotiator must not only strategically manage his own actions but those of the other negotiator as well. This is challenging enough when the other negotiator has objectively and reasonably evaluated his BATNA, WATNA, and MLATNA. The negotiation becomes even more difficult for you, however, if the other negotiator is overly optimistic about his BATNA, WATNA, and MLATNA.

For example, suppose there was a general contractor named Benjamin. He successfully bid on a project for construction of a three-story office building. As is customary in the commercial construction trade, Benjamin received bids from electrical, painting, plumbing, plaster, carpentry, and tile subcontractors. Halfway through the project, right when he needed to have the floor tile installed, the tile and flooring subcontractor told him he was held up on another job. Benjamin was furious because this would create scheduling problems with the other subcontractors, thus delaying completion of the project. The tile subcontractor had many other jobs, so if he lost this one it would not be a big problem financially. Therefore, he had a realistic sense of his BATNA and WATNA. His MLATNA was pretty good, too: If he lost this job, he could probably replace it with

> ## Negotiating Tip
>
> The effective negotiator must not only strategically manage his own actions but those of the other negotiator as well. The negotiation becomes more difficult if the other negotiator is overly optimistic about his BATNA, WATNA, and MLATNA.

a similar job. Ideally, the tile subcontractor would try to work out the scheduling problem with Benjamin and retain the job.

Benjamin, on the other hand, badly misjudged his BATNA, WATNA, and MLATNA. Benjamin assumed that he could find another tile subcontractor to come in on short notice to do the job at the same price. So, he fired the tile subcontractor he had. Unfortunately, he could not find a replacement tile subcontractor to start the job any sooner than six weeks later, and all the tile subcontractors he located bid the job at substantially more than the one he already had. In this instance, Benjamin unrealistically assessed his BATNA, WATNA, and MLATNA. The tile subcontractor he fired did not. Benjamin blew it, the project was delayed anyway, and he paid more to have the tile work completed than if he had tried to work something out with the existing tile subcontractor.

When two negotiators are not on the same page about the evaluation of risk, they are not likely to reach agreement. Deals are reached when both negotiators are evaluating the costs and benefits of reaching agreement similarly. Successful business negotiators large and small are masters at objectively estimating their BATNAs, WATNAs, and MLATNAs.

Recommended Solution

Provide objective, reliable information that can be readily verified by the other negotiator. In the context of settlement negotiations in lawsuits, this kind of information includes prior jury verdicts and judgments in the jurisdiction where the case will be tried. In real estate and business negotiations, such information includes appraisals by neutral and well-respected appraisers. In consumer transactions, this means giving the customer independent and reliable information about the availability and cost of a product or service. Resorting to reliable outside sources of information is one of the most effective ways of overcoming the challenge to agreement posed by negotiators with significantly mismatched expectations about their respective BATNAs, WATNAs, and MLATNAs.

In the construction project discussed above, all the tile subcontractor had to do to keep a satisfied client was to inform Benjamin that all reputable local tile and flooring subcontractors were booked up, and that any of them would likely bid the job at the same or higher price. He could invite Benjamin to check it out. Benjamin would have found out in short order that the tile subcontractor was right, and then the issue of the job delay might have been worked out. By effectively managing Benjamin's unrealistic assessment of his alternatives, the tile subcontractor could have retained a good business relationship and made more money. Benjamin and the tile subcontractor could have reached a compromise calling for a brief delay and a price adjustment on the subcontract. Both negotiators could have achieved a mutually acceptable agreement by virtue of the tile subcontractor's strategic management of the situation. Sometimes, the smart business negotiator needs to help the other negotiator accurately assess his alternatives away from the table. Most often, you can do that by making objective and reliable information available to the other negotiator.

Conflict and Distrust

Conflict

Negotiations can give rise to conflicts of varying causes, intensities, and consequences. Conflict in a negotiation can be the result of misunderstanding, differing personalities, or mismatched communication styles. Conflict can also arise when the underlying interests of the negotiators are opposed, as when they both need the same thing very badly and there is not enough of that thing to share satisfactorily. Conflict has many causes. Its effects on negotiations, however, are predictable and profound. When conflict emerges in a negotiation, a deal that could have been closed is lost. Worse, the conflict may escalate and harm personal or business relationships.

When conflict exists, negotiating can be very difficult and people do things that are not strategic. Consider the following (fictional) tale of William, the chief financial officer of a commercial film processing company, STPicCorp. William is an experienced financial professional, and he has been the CFO of STPicCorp for five years. William joined the company when it was on the verge of bankruptcy and he has been instrumental in its resurrection to profitability. William is exceptionally hard working and demanding.

William enjoys his work, but he cannot stand STPicCorp's president, Elaine. William feels that Elaine, who is very self-confident but has less years of experience than William, does not treat him with the appropriate degree of respect. In the last two years, Elaine has made decisions affecting William without consulting him. For instance, Elaine has re-assigned one of William's staff to another division without first consulting William. Most recently, Elaine approved a budget that called for the cancellation of the firm's subscription to a financial software update program that William values very highly. Again, Elaine did not consult William beforehand. When William e-mailed Elaine to ask why the software updates were being discontinued, and why he had not been consulted beforehand,

> **Negotiating Tip**
>
> Conflict has many causes. Conflict in a negotiation can be the result of misunderstanding, differing personalities, or mismatched communication styles. Conflict can also arise when the underlying interests of the negotiators are opposed.

Elaine told him via e-mail, "Budget had to be submitted to board. No time to discuss. On my way to meeting with chairman. We can discuss later."

This most recent incident was the last straw. William does not want to leave STPicCorp, but he simply cannot tolerate Elaine any longer. He is strongly considering a new position with STPicCorp's main competitor, TruPhilmCo. This move would be a major betrayal for Bert Favorsheim, the founder of STPicCorp and the person who hired William. But what else can William do? "How do you negotiate with someone like Elaine?" he asks himself. Better just to leave and deal with it that way.

For her part, Elaine thinks William is humorless and arrogant. William and Elaine joined STPicCorp at the same time as part of a new management team assigned to turn the company around. They worked very long hours in the first two years, so she spent considerable time with William. Elaine is very outgoing and personable. Her strengths are presentation and fostering relationships, particularly with customers, vendors, and the board. William, on the other hand, is very curt, short, and often upsets those same constituencies. Elaine has no doubt William is the best financial officer with whom she has ever worked, and he is a big reason the company is now profitable. Still, she feels William is dismissive of her ideas and leadership, and she thinks he is a misogynist. William is liked by the board, particularly Bert Favorsheim, the founder and chairman. Elaine has a very good relationship with Bert, however, and feels he might back her up if she recommended that William leave. Elaine wishes to avoid that result, though, and she is at a loss to figure out how to deal with the situation. "How can you negotiate with someone so closed and unfriendly as William?" she asks herself.

Like most people in conflict, William and Elaine are so upset with the situation they assume that ending the working relationship will make them feel better. William would prefer to stay with STPicCorp, a company he loves, doing work he enjoys, and being paid well. Elaine also wants to stay at STPicCorp, and she would prefer to retain a CFO as talented as William. Both William and Elaine derive tremendous benefit from their working relationship. Unfortunately, neither William nor Elaine is thinking strategically about how to deal with the situation. Otherwise, they might consider ways of negotiating a continuation of their working relationship while at the same addressing their interpersonal concerns.

William and Elaine, however, did not do that. After more than a year of not talking directly with each other and letting their internal dissatisfaction simmer, William quit STPicCorp to join its chief competitor, TruPhilmCo. Bert Favorsheim, the founder and chairman of the board, is furious, particularly with Elaine for letting it happen. Elaine's position with the board has been weakened, and the company has lost a valuable CFO. William is not any happier. He dislikes the corporate culture at TruPhilmCo and the financial management structure is dated and inefficient. He wishes he were still at STPicCorp, but that is impossible now. Neither Elaine nor William got what they wanted or needed. That is how failing to manage conflict and distrust can create bad deals.

Unmanaged, conflict festers and interferes with strategic negotiating. Fortunately, there are effective approaches to working through conflict to try and reach better deals.

Recommended Solutions

There are many approaches to managing conflict in the course of negotiating, any of which, alone or in combination, may be effective:

1. Be soft on the people, hard on the issue, i.e., separate the people from the problem and adjust your words accordingly.

William and Elaine could have attempted a dialogue about what was bothering them, rather than privately brooding about their mutual contempt. The problem is creating an opening for such dialogue. William might approach Elaine one morning (when she was not in a rush) and say, "Elaine, can we find a convenient time today or tomorrow to have a talk?" Or Elaine could initiate the discussion with a similar opening. Beginning with an acknowledgment of tension may also help to create a discussion that is "soft on the people." Elaine might start by saying, "William, I value your contributions to the company tremendously. I've been feeling, however, like you're upset with me, and I know I've been upset with you. Rather than letting these feelings interfere with our working relationship, I thought we might try to get them on the table and figure out how we can make things better between us. Can we get together for lunch this week and try to work things out?" A similar opening would work well for William.

Being "soft on the people" is just a way of describing the use of calming, reassuring language to begin a discussion about difficult feelings, beliefs, or emotions that need to be resolved in order for a negotiation to be fruitful.

2. Words are powerful in both good and bad ways, so manage your language in a neutral and positive way.

William could respond to Elaine's "soft on the people" overture by angrily saying, "Unless you're here to apologize, I'm not interested. You're rude and inconsiderate, and I'm through trying to deal with you." This would invite Elaine to be defensive and retaliate with an assertion of her power and control, such as "Fine. I was trying to figure out if there was a way we could continue working together, but I guess there is not!"

Language—your choice of words—is power. But the power of words is a lot like fire; it can cook and warm, or it can burn and destroy. Think of the words you use when you are upset or angry the same way. You need to make thoughtful choices about your words at critical moments. Once words come out, try taking them back. E-mail is a great example of the permanence of the word spoken in anger. At least with the spoken word, memories and anger may fade. The written word, however, lasts forever. It is there in print as a constant reminder of how you lost your cool.

Even though William is upset, he could respond to Elaine's inquiry by saying, "I'm glad you're willing to talk with me about this. I've been very upset about some things." This invites dialogue. Lashing out in an angry, aggressive way invites escalation and termination of dialogue. The choice is always yours. Keep your eyes on the prize at all times: getting better deals means managing your emotions, communicating effectively, and learning information. Words can help or hurt your goals.

3. Be clear and consistent to avoid frustrating the other negotiator.

Elaine should not begin the discussion with a cooperative opening, and then respond angrily when William shares what he's thinking. "I feel like you don't treat me with the kind of respect I feel I am due," William might say. Elaine should respond to this with something like, "If there is anything I've done to make you feel that way, please let me know, and I apologize. I value your work and I do respect you." Being "soft on the people" means not shutting the door when the other negotiator tells you something you do not want to hear. Remember, the strategic negotiator is trying to gather information to diagnose the source of the conflict, so that she can determine the best approach to resolving it and reaching a deal.

4. State all terms, conditions, and requirements of the deal up front, rather than adding them on later.

Suppose Elaine and William are good strategic negotiators, and they use "soft on the people" language to discuss their personal differences. Things are progressing well, and they negotiate a way to interact with each other more effectively. As they are about to shake hands on a new working relationship, William asks, "Oh, by the way, I'm presenting a request for a $50,000 increase in my salary to Bert; will you support me on that?" Elaine may feel betrayed by such a competitive move at the end of a cooperative negotiation. William may undermine the cooperative working relationship he was trying to create with Elaine. Sometimes the "add-on"—asking for a significant concession after an agreement in principle has been reached—destroys the other negotiator's trust you have worked very hard to create.

5. If the negotiators are not comfortable using the same language, retain an interpreter for assistance.

If William were Japanese and Elaine were American, in addition to cultural and gender challenges, there would be language concerns. To minimize misunderstanding, a competent interpreter should always be used where both negotiators are not comfortable in the language being used to conduct the negotiation.

6. When positions collide, focus on both negotiators' underlying interests and the ways they can be satisfied.

In the example of William and Elaine, both negotiators should avoid reacting angrily to each other, and they should use techniques to focus their conversation on their shared underlying interests. For instance, if Elaine reacts angrily to William's statement that she should have consulted him before canceling the software update subscription, William might say, "Elaine, I'm not suggesting that you are not entitled to make budget recommendations based on your best judgment. That's what you're paid to do, and I respect your judgment. I'm just saying that, since I am the CFO, you and I should be communicating about important decisions affecting the company's financial management. This software update is one of those things I believe we should be communicating about as part of a healthy working relationship." Notice that William brings the conversation away from fault and toward a shared process necessary to their common underlying interest—working effectively with each other. This is where successful negotiators shine.

7. Remember Axelrod's Theory: Demonstrate cooperativeness, but be prepared to protect yourself by being competitive when you need to do so.

If Elaine exhibits cooperation by beginning the negotiation with "soft on the people" language, and William responds competitively, such as, "I think I'll take it up with Bert and see what he thinks about your style of dealing with people," Elaine has a choice. She can ignore the comment, or she can respond competitively, such as "That's an option, William, but Bert might not think we're too competent if we are both asking him to resolve a problem we aren't able to deal with." This competitive response equalizes the power and says, "I can play that game, too, but it won't get us what we need."

8. *Avoid attributing bad intent or motive to something the other negotiator says or does; the fact is you do not know the thoughts of anyone other than yourself.*

Elaine may feel that William is arrogant and disrespects her authority because she is a woman. William may feel that Elaine is power hungry and simply wants him to look bad so she can take over the company. Both are completely wrong about the other; they are just having an interpersonal conflict that is made worse by their personalities, communication styles, and positions of power. If either Elaine or William acted on their uncharitable beliefs about each other, it could get ugly very quickly. Good negotiators understand that they do not know what is in the other negotiator's head. It is their job to find out. When you want to fly off the handle because of your own fears, assume that the other negotiator may not be thinking what you think she thinks. You might be the only person thinking what you are thinking. That is food for thought.

9. *If it is too difficult to deal with the other negotiator, consider and use your power to get what you need from someone else and walk away.*

If Elaine is unreasonable and refuses to negotiate cooperatively with William, William can achieve power in the conversation by seeking the assistance of a superior, Bert, the chairman of the board. Seeking outside power sources—the legal process, a superior, another buyer or seller—is an effective way of dealing with a situation that is not made better by your deft management of communication.

10. *Avoid threats, insults, or sarcasm.*

Does it really need saying that you should not lose it and be threatening, insulting or sarcastic? Yes, it does, because no matter how obvious this directive is, we violate it every day. Strategic self management means avoiding this type of behavior at all costs. Talk about what you need and why, what you believe and why, what has upset you and why. That's what being "soft on the people, hard on the issue" is all about. When you lose control, someone else will claim it. That person is likely to be the other negotiator. Do not give up your power to the other negotiator by losing your temper.

11. To avoid escalating the conflict into a lawsuit, seek the help of a trained, experienced, and skilled mediator to assist the negotiation.

If the conflict is serious enough to potentially result in a lawsuit, whatever else you do, seek the advice of a trained, experienced, and licensed attorney who has knowledge of and expertise in the subject. Contact your local bar association for a referral to an attorney, or obtain a referral from another local business owner.

Whether you have obtained the advice of a lawyer or not, however, you can take the initiative in managing conflict and finding a way to negotiate through it by using a process called mediation. As mentioned previously, mediation is a process in which the parties seek the assistance of a neutral and impartial third person—the mediator—to assist them in negotiating a resolution to the conflict. Businesses use mediation all the time when conflict and distrust pose significant barriers to negotiating effectively. Mediation can play an important role in de-escalating conflict in the human resources arena, in which miscommunication, anger, and distrust can not only create disharmony in the workplace but the probability of employment litigation. These problems are not good for business.

For example, Bert, the chairman of the board of STPicCorp, could see that the conflict between William and Elaine, two highly valued executives, is bad for the well being of the company. Bert might insist that a mediator be called in to assist William and Elaine in negotiating a de-escalation of their conflict and a workable long-term agreement that bolsters their business relationship. That is an attractive alternative for the business compared to losing either William or Elaine, or, worse, a lawsuit by one or the other. Letting conflicts fester within the workplace is not a sound business strategy.

12. If the other negotiator has consulted with a lawyer, you should do so as well.

If the other negotiator obtains a lawyer, she has a significant power advantage if you do not do so yourself. Remember, strategic negotiators obtain information, and information is power. A lawyer helps you make informed decisions, which increases your power in the negotiation. To avoid escalating the conflict unnecessarily, be clear with your attorney that you wish to level the playing field and have sound advice, not make a problem worse. Avoid bombastic lawyers who seem incapable of calming the situation down. Instead, choose an experienced attorney with a reputation for being forceful when she needs to be, but effective at quietly working out problems in the business environment. Again, the best way to find an effective lawyer to help you work out these situations is by asking colleagues for referrals.

13. Avoid offering anything you are not confident you can deliver.

Nothing destroys trust faster than promising something that does not turn out to be true. It is natural for us to make promises with all the best intentions in the world, but to exceed what we can reasonably deliver. With conflict, intentions are less important than results. Only promise what you can safely deliver.

For example, suppose that William and Elaine reach an agreement in which Elaine will meet and confer with William well in advance of any recommendation to the board to make budgetary or staff changes affecting William's operations. If Elaine does not manage her time well, and does not make a concerted effort to create the time to put this agreement into effect, she is likely to not follow through on her promise. She may contact William a day before a board meeting in which she plans to seek the board's approval for a staff reduction that affects William's operations. William may respond by distrusting Elaine's motives and feeling disrespected, an escalation of the conflict. Broken promises kill deals; fulfilled promises earn trust. It is as simple as that.

14. Leave the other negotiator with an opportunity to save face, whether you like doing so or not.

If the other negotiator has truly made a mistake or is at fault, but the negotiation is producing a satisfactory agreement, give the other negotiator a chance to save face. This is particularly true when dealing with a negotiator from a culture in which saving face is very important. Even though Elaine was wrong to not consult William before canceling the software update, William would do well to let it go if his negotiation with Elaine produces a better deal. Proving yourself right has less value sometimes than working out a really great deal.

15. Make the other negotiator feel like a winner by convincing him that you are "giving up" and that he is "winning."

If Elaine is a sophisticated negotiator, she will make something of a show of giving in to William's superior negotiating skill. Elaine may have to bite her tongue to do so, but she will be employing an age-old wisdom of negotiating: When you win something big, pretend that you have given up something bigger and that your negotiating partner has won the game. Great negotiators do this to get better deals every day.

Setting this situation up takes patience and timing. For example, William may propose that no budgetary decisions be made without his express approval. Elaine does not want to give William veto power, but she knows that a simple "no" invites a power struggle with William, and she wants to avoid that. So Elaine might hesitate an uncomfortably long time, and then propose that she will agree that William is important to any budget decisions affecting his operations, and that Elaine will agree to consult with William about any such budgetary issues before they are proposed to the board. Elaine will further agree to seek agreement with William as the ideal goal of their meeting on budgetary issues before proposing any changes to the board. Notice that Elaine is conceding some power to William, but not all of it. And she has deftly avoided giving William veto power. Instead, all she has done is agree to *try* to reach agreement with him before she submits any budget proposals to the board. William will feel like the winner, and Elaine retains all of her options in the event she cannot work out a budget issue with William.

16. Consider making an important concession as a peace offering.

When negotiators have experienced conflict, a peace offering carries huge symbolic significance and can generate reciprocal concessions. For example,

William might signal to Elaine that he respects her authority and wants to make peace. So William might concede to Elaine the power of making budget presentations to the board without William being present in exchange for Elaine's concession that she needs to confer with William concerning budgetary matters beforehand. "I trust you, Elaine; I don't need to be there if we have already talked about the budget," is the message William sends by making this concession. These peace offerings can be tremendously powerful remedies for conflict, as long as they are reciprocated and respected.

17. Take a break to get some fresh air and think things over, particularly when you are getting angry.

In any conflict situation, it is best to take a deep breath, clear your mind, and consider your strategic response. All strategic negotiators do this. Sometimes, it is hard to calm down and think strategically unless you remove yourself from the situation by taking a break. For example, William might have said to Elaine at the beginning of their conflict, "You're arrogant and out of touch with what's really going on in this company." People say things like that when they are angry. William is thinking, "How dare you submit a budget that affects me without consulting with me first?" but he has not fashioned his thinking in that way yet. If Elaine is a strategic negotiator, she knows she needs to calm down before making the next move, so she might say to William, "I need to think about what you've said," or something to that effect, and find a graceful way of taking a break.

After calming down, she can come back to the conversation with questions designed to obtain information, such as "I would like to understand why there is such tension between us. What is your perspective about what's going on? I'd like to know what you think." Notice that Elaine has provided some space for her strategic thinking to overcome her emotional response. That is what the best negotiators do.

18. Focus on the common problem both negotiators can agree they must solve.

Remember, the soul of cooperative negotiating is that both negotiators have made the strategic decision that they have more to gain by working together than by competing against each other. If both Elaine and William are strategic negotiators, they will manage their communication to focus on the common problem or goals they share. Often, however, only one of the negotiators is thinking strategically; the other needs to be brought to the same way of approaching the negotiation.

For example, Elaine might be very angry at William's suggestion that Elaine needs to consult with William on important budgetary decisions. She sees William's insistence on this as undermining her authority as president of the company. William can be sensitive to this concern by reassuring Elaine that he respects her leadership of the company, but that they have the common goal of working as a team. This focus on teamwork is one of the most effective ways of channeling a negotiation to common problem solving. William can focus the negotiation this way by saying, "Elaine, you're the president, and I respect your leadership and the need for you to manage accordingly. However, I'm the chief financial officer, and we need to work together as a team. It's important to the company that we are on the same page. How can we create that kind of teamwork?"

Distrust

Distrust is the great killer of deals and the frequent companion of conflict. Trust takes a long time to acquire, but it can be destroyed in the blink of an eye, and, once lost, can only be regained over time, if at all. This is not just a maxim of morality and ethics; it is a description of human nature, and a wisdom of business. When we cannot trust the other negotiator, or vice versa, the deal suffers. If A promises to do something, can B rely on that promise? Will it be done? If B doubts the promise, B may be tempted to negotiate for additional terms that compensate for this uncertainty. A might not like those terms, many of which seem to plan for failure rather than success. B's distrust then becomes A's distrust, and the cycle goes on from there.

> **Negotiating Tip**
>
> Trust takes a long time to acquire, but it can be destroyed in the blink of an eye, and, once lost, can be difficult or impossible to regain. This is not just a maxim of morality and ethics; it is a description of human nature, and a wisdom of business.

Recommended Solutions

Consider the following ways in which negotiators deal with issues of trust in a negotiation:

- Reaffirm the shared purpose of the negotiation, including a common underlying interest to be met or a common problem to be solved.
- Provide proof or verification of disputed information.
- Demonstrate trustworthiness by agreeing to do something and then doing it.
- Obtain an outside opinion from a credible source.
- Focus on shared beliefs, experiences, background, and values (positive association).
- Discourage bias, stereotypes, and generalizations (negative association).
- Obtain the assistance of a trained, experienced, and skilled mediator to facilitate the negotiation.
- Make an honest and sincere apology for any statement or action that has contributed to the lack of trust.
- If you are wrong, try to make it right.

Conflict and distrust arise frequently, but they can be effectively managed using the above techniques. Ultimately, if the deal is worth closing, the strategic negotiator must be prepared to assess and manage any and all impediments to negotiation and agreement. That is how the best negotiators earn their success.

The Law

As we discussed in the previous chapter, there are instances in which the law limits the behavior of the negotiator and the type of agreement that may be reached. The problem is that frequently people negotiate with little or no knowledge or awareness of the law, thus exposing their negotiations and agreements to the risk of liability and litigation.

Recommended Solutions

- If you are a commercial seller of goods or services, be aware of all federal and state laws, rules and regulations affecting your negotiation behavior and agreements, including those that require or prohibit statements, representations, warranties, promises, and disclosures. Trade associations and publications, as well as governmental agencies, provide this information free of charge.

> ### Negotiating Tip
>
> Unfortunately, people often negotiate with little or no knowledge or awareness of the law, thus exposing their negotiations and agreements to the risk of liability and litigation.

- Be particularly careful if you are an executor of a probate estate, a trustee of a trust, or a guardian or conservator of an elderly person, dependent adult, or child. There are many legal limits and implications of the actions of these persons, including fiduciary duties and court supervision. You are best advised to consult with a trained, experienced, and licensed attorney where you have these legal responsibilities.
- Avoid untruthful statements of material fact about any goods, services, or property you are negotiating. In most instances, such dishonesty is fraudulent and may expose you to civil or criminal liability.
- Consult with experienced and skilled tax professionals, attorneys, real estate professionals, and other experts concerning any applicable legal requirements. Do not leave yourself in the dark.
- When in doubt, find out! Ignorance of the law is never an excuse.

Power Imbalance

Relationship

Every personal, business, or social relationship has implications of power between the parties to the relationship. In some instances, the parties' power is balanced. An example of this is two businesses of approximately equal size and economic strength. Another example is a seller and prospective buyer of commercial goods or products in an open market. In many instances, however, one party in a relationship may have more power than the other. For example, employers typically have more power in the employment relationship than the employee, unless the employee is highly valued and the market demand for his services is great. A large commercial real estate developer typically enjoys more power than the construction sub-contractors who compete with each other to work on the developer's projects. In personal relationships, such as those between spouses, there is nearly always an imbalance of power of some sort.

Recommended Solutions

It is very difficult to remedy a power imbalance in a business or personal relationship. In a business relationship, one solution is for the less powerful party to find power outside the relationship, for example, by entering into a different relationship with another negotiating partner. Typically, leaving the relationship is the most powerful way of remedying an imbalance of power. The problem is that the less powerful negotiator may not have that luxury. As long as the relationship continues, the imbalance will continue. More powerful negotiators do not readily give their power away.

Status

People may acquire superior power in a negotiation by virtue of their social status. For example, in many cultures, the elderly enjoy superior power to younger people. Wealth may also be a social status conferring superior negotiating power.

Recommended Solutions

Where culture confers superior power to a negotiator because of status, there is no conventional means for the less powerful negotiator to balance the power. In such instances, the negotiation will be canted in favor of the more powerful person, and that is accepted in the culture. In some countries, for example, the negotiation between a large commercial general contractor and a concrete subcontractor concerning construction of a hotel is unavoidably power imbalanced. In the particular culture, it would be unheard of for the subcontractor to threaten to work with another general contractor, and the subcontractor must submit to a lopsided deal because of the status of the general contractor. In these cultures, the more powerful party is expected to and does reciprocate to some extent by providing steady work to loyal, less powerful parties.

Unfortunately, power imbalance in these cultures also perpetuates ruthless exploitation of less powerful interests by more powerful ones.

Where wealth or some other status factor confers power, the less powerful negotiator gains power by having options away from the table. Here is a fictional example. There is a significant power imbalance between an immigrant landscaper, who we will call James, and his employer, a successful film producer who we will call Mr. Farnsworth. The balance shifts quickly once James is offered employment exclusively with Mr. Farnsworth's wealthy neighbor, Ms. Becker, a competing producer. James now has power. He might double his money by playing both wealthy clients against each other.

> **Definition**
>
> Status is the relative position or standing of persons in a society. Status is determined by factors such as wealth, age, social standing, and level of authority in a business.

External

A negotiator may acquire power outside the negotiation. For example, one source of power is the threat or reality of a lawsuit. The power of the court to order damages or issue an injunction can confer significant power on a negotiator. Other external sources of power include partnering with more powerful allies, including businesses, advocacy organizations, or governmental agencies. Getting a lawyer is an immediate way of accessing an external power source.

Recommended Solutions

The less powerful negotiator can reach out to external power sources, too. A cross-action in a lawsuit is a typical means of doing so, as are acquiring powerful allies, or seeking the assistance of governmental agencies. Obtaining the assistance of an attorney is a way of accessing an external source of substantial power. Unfortunately, when one does so, one risks an escalation of any conflict in the negotiation.

To use another fictional example, Wilhelmina owns a pizza franchise. The franchisor, a nationwide chain of pizza restaurants, requires that Wilhelmina, like all other franchisees, purchase supplies and food stuffs from the franchisor exclusively at inflated prices. After a year or so of this, Wilhelmina wants to negotiate a better deal with the franchisor. The large company laughs at Wilhelmina. It stops laughing the day that Wilhelmina's lawyer writes to the company suggesting that its contract is void because it violates federal anti-trust laws. Wilhelmina, the small franchisee, has suddenly gained power in the negotiation with a credible threat of valid litigation to void an illegal contractual provision. The pizza franchisor agrees to negotiate the cost of the supplies Wilhelmina is required to purchase. The power imbalance has been corrected for the moment.

BATNA/MLATNA

Whenever a negotiator has better options away from the table than the options at the table—that is real power.

Recommended Solutions

None. A person who has better options away from the table has no reason to stay. Therefore, the less powerful negotiator has only two choices: give in or not do the deal.

Fear/Intimidation

Often, a negotiator acquires power by verbal or physical threats and intimidation, or by virtue of a prior history of force, violence, threat, or fear against the less powerful negotiator. In family law disputes, a history of domestic violence can create a serious power imbalance between spouses negotiating property division or child custody issues.

Recommended Solutions

If physical or emotional abuse or violence has been a feature of the negotiators' interactions, direct negotiation between the parties must be avoided. Instead, negotiations should be conducted through legal representatives, most typically attorneys. Additionally, the less powerful negotiator can seek external sources of power, including the assistance of counsel, police, or the court system.

If a negotiator's behavior does not rise to this level, but the negotiator is using the tactics of bullying or intimidation, as we discussed in Chapter Four, identify the tactic, assess your response, and respond strategically. Frequently, your best move is to confront the tactic with the other negotiator and then negotiate process. For example, if the other negotiator tries to bully you by getting in your face and using assertive and intimidating language, you can tell him to back off, and you can ask him whether he wants to do a deal with you. If so, he will need to take a different approach. That can work wonders in changing an intimidating tactic into a more cooperative approach.

The above list of common problems and recommended solutions is not meant to be exhaustive, but it is simply an aid to becoming a more effective negotiator. Dealing with the problems that arise in negotiations involves a fundamentally strategic decision on your part: How do you get an agreement that meets your needs, or are you better served by meeting your needs some other way? As with all disciplines, effective strategic negotiation takes trial and error. Only with experience can a negotiator learn techniques for overcoming the many problems that can arise in negotiations.

All of the approaches discussed above have a common denominator: The strategic negotiator identifies the problem, diagnoses its cause, and crafts a strategy for dealing with the problem. At all stages in the negotiation process, you get better deals—even by not getting any deal at all—by being the driver, not the passenger. Manage or be managed. You have the choice of how to respond to what the other negotiator does. Being a good driver means knowing how to adjust to the many different hazards on the road to your destination.

> **Negotiating Tip**
>
> The strategic negotiator identifies the problem, diagnoses its cause, and crafts a strategy for dealing with the problem. At all stages in the negotiation process, you get better deals by being the driver, not the passenger. Being a good driver means knowing how to adjust to the many different hazards on the road to your destination.

Key Points to Remember: Chapter 7

1. Avoid or minimize problems caused by absent decision makers.

2. Obtain accurate, objective information upon which to base your decisions.

3. Understand and adjust to differing communication processing styles.

4. Be realistic, not overly optimistic, in estimating your BATNA, WATNA, and MLATNA.

5. Offer credible, objectively verifiable information to the other negotiator if he has an unrealistic estimate of his BATNA, WATNA, and MLATNA.

6. Manage conflict and distrust through cooperative negotiating techniques.

7. Do not let conflict manage you.

8. Ignorance of the law is no excuse; be informed, and seek the advice of an attorney when in doubt.

9. Whenever possible, balance power by negotiating with someone else, walking away, obtaining a lawyer, seeking court intervention, or allying with a powerful partner.

10. When problems arise in the negotiation, be the driver—not the passenger.

CHAPTER 8

Driving to Your Destination

There is so much more that can be written about how to negotiate better deals! This book is by no means an exhaustive discussion of all the different things negotiators do to be successful. No such book can be written. The best negotiators learn by trial and error, but there is one thing they all know that we have emphasized in various ways throughout this book: You get better deals by driving the negotiation to the destination that serves your needs the best. You can do that by being strategically competitive or cooperative, or a little bit of both; it all depends on what you are trying to achieve in the negotiation. The key is managing yourself and encouraging the other negotiator to make the decisions that advance the negotiation toward the desired agreement. Preparation, patience, self-discipline, attention to language, and good listening are the tools strategic negotiators use to get better deals. You can do the same.

Negotiating can be fun, but we must give ourselves permission to enjoy it. Too often we fear negotiating, often because we have too readily accepted the role of passenger and not driver. Perhaps we feel that being a better negotiator is not who we are, but that is simply our lack of confidence speaking. We make choices whether to negotiate strategically or not, whether to be the driver or the passenger. This book is all about encouraging you to exercise that power of choice to negotiate better deals. In the business world, whether you own a corner grocery store or a Fortune 500 company, being the driver rather than the passenger in your negotiations is the difference between increasing and decreasing your profit margin. Growth and success come from maximizing profit, not minimizing it.

> **Negotiating Tip**
>
> Being a strategic negotiator, a driver, is innate; it's a natural part of who we are, whether we realize it or not.

Being a strategic negotiator, a driver, is innate; it is a natural part of who we are, whether we realize it or not. Consider a classic negotiation between one of the authors and his eight-year-old daughter. The author's daughter was given the privilege of staying up until 9 p.m. She loves to read, and was really into her book when Dad walked in and said, "Time for lights out, sweetie." The daughter looked heartbroken, and sweetly asked, "Can I have 15 more minutes, pleeeeease?" Dad said, "No, hon, it's time for lights out." His daughter pleaded her case. "I'm at a really exciting part of the book, ten more minutes, and I'll put the light out, pleeeeeeeeeeeeeeeease?" Dad, a negotiation professional and educator, answered, "Okay, five minutes, then lights out." His daughter, quite encouraged, asked, "Nine minutes?" Dad held firm, "Not one second past seven minutes." His daughter seemed pleased. "Okay."

The daughter did not read this book, or attend the authors' classes, or study the many articles and books written on the subject of negotiation. Yet this child knew intuitively, as all children do, how to negotiate. Perhaps our life experiences and personalities divorce us from the exuberant freedom with which we naturally negotiated as children. But inside each of us is the power to achieve what we need, and negotiating is the way to unleash it. We simply have lost touch with our inner power, that voice that encouraged the author's daughter to negotiate for a better deal.

If this book has done nothing more than encourage you to feel liberated to embrace negotiating as a necessary means of achieving what you need in business and life, then we have succeeded. As with all skills, negotiating can be done wisely or foolishly, helpfully or hurtfully. The choice, as we have said all along, is up to you. We hope this book has helped you to be the best negotiator you can be. Good luck.

Glossary

Agreement: The objective of a negotiation. An agreement may be written or it may be oral. Sometimes referred to as the "deal."

Anchoring: A principle of psychology in which the negotiator encourages the other negotiator to be less risk tolerant and accept a final proposal by characterizing it as a gain rather than a loss. Anchoring involves the use of language in presenting the final offer by summarizing the gains the other negotiator has achieved, thus influencing the other negotiator to accept the offer.

Axelrod's Theory of Avoiding Exploitation: A four-step approach to assist negotiators in avoiding exploitation by a competitive negotiator. In this approach, the negotiator starts off competitively and then alternates between competitive and cooperative moves during the negotiation to encourage cooperation by the other negotiator.

BATNA: "Best Alternative to Negotiated Agreement." This is the best-case scenario available to the negotiator if he or she does not reach agreement in the negotiation. Typically, a BATNA means the best possible outcome if the negotiator negotiates with someone else or goes to court.

Bluffing: A negotiator's actions that pretend that the negotiator has more leverage or options than her or she has. The purpose of bluffing is to encourage the other negotiator to make concessions.

Bottom Line: The least desirable outcome a negotiator will accept and feel that the negotiation is satisfactory. A negotiator's bottom line is that point beyond which the negotiator will not negotiate any further. Otherwise known as the "walk-away point."

Brainstorming: A step in the cooperative negotiating (or integrative bargaining) process in which the negotiators try to create options that have the potential for mutual gain.

Competition: A negotiator's effort to claim more value than the other negotiator in the negotiation. When a negotiator competes for the greatest share of the value being negotiated, his gains are achieved only when the other negotiator makes a corresponding concession or loss. The opposite of cooperation.

Competitive Negotiating: A process of negotiating in which both negotiators try to claim the largest share of whatever value is being negotiated. The timing and size of concessions in competitive negotiating is predictable and, therefore, highly manageable. Competitive negotiating typically involves the strategic sending of signals to the other negotiator to signify the ease or difficulty with which the negotiator makes concessions. Otherwise known as "distributive bargaining" or "positional negotiating."

Concessions: An offer or proposal that gives something of value to the other negotiator. It is the exchange of concessions that fuels the negotiating dance.

Cooperation: A negotiator's effort to create value by negotiating in a way that recognizes that neither negotiator needs to lose in order for both negotiators to meet their needs. The opposite of competition.

Cooperative Negotiating: A process of negotiating in which both negotiators accept that their goal is to meet each other's needs in reaching agreement. Otherwise known as "integrative bargaining" or "win/win" negotiation. Unlike competitive negotiating, cooperative negotiating is achieved by the use of cooperative language, rapport, and collaborative problem solving in an attempt to reach agreement. Cooperative negotiating requires some degree of trust between negotiators in order to achieve a durable agreement.

(The) Dance: The back-and-forth between the negotiators that typifies the negotiation itself. This is the process by which negotiators exchange proposals or concessions in negotiating a deal. The dance begins with the first offer or proposal, and it continues so long as the negotiators exchange offers or proposals. The dance ends when the negotiators reach an agreement or when they conclude that they cannot reach an agreement.

Distributive Bargaining: The same thing as "competitive negotiating." Negotiating for the biggest slice of the pie.

Durable Agreement: A lasting agreement that the negotiators will honor and fulfill. A durable agreement is achieved if the negotiating process and the agreement satisfy the negotiators' core needs and interests.

Exploitation: One negotiator taking advantage of the other. Typically, exploitation occurs when a negotiator gives up too much value in a negotiation. This usually happens when one negotiator is being cooperative and the other negotiator is being competitive. Axelrod's Theory of Avoiding Exploitation suggests a strategic approach that negotiators take to avoid this result.

Fixed Pie or Fixed Pie of Value: A term used in describing competitive negotiating that signifies the limited resource over which the negotiators are competing to claim the biggest share or "slice."

Fraud: The intentional or negligent misstatement of a material fact (or the intentional or negligent failure to disclose a material fact when one has the legal duty to make such disclosure) that induces the other negotiator to enter into an agreement and that causes harm to the other negotiator. Fraudulent conduct can be prosecuted criminally and it can give rise to civil liability, including punitive damages in extreme cases.

Integrative Bargaining: The same thing as "cooperative negotiating." Negotiating for shared or mutual gain.

Interest: A negotiator's underlying reason why she takes a position in a negotiation. Typically, an interest is a need, desire, or objective the negotiator is trying to achieve in the negotiation. If the negotiation does not meet the negotiator's underlying interests, it is not likely to produce a durable agreement.

Issue: The concrete, tangible thing that is the subject of the negotiation. The negotiators each take positions concerning how the issue shall be resolved by agreement.

Linkage: The combining together of different tangible things, different pies of value, in order to make agreement easier. Examples of linkage include payment terms, escrow periods, and the like.

Magnetic Pull Effect: A description of the power of opening offers to manage the other negotiator's expectations about what kind of a deal can be achieved. Examples include the Manufacturer's Suggested Retail price sticker on a new car or appliance.

Managing Expectations: Getting the other negotiator to do what you need him or her to do in the negotiation. This is done by the strategic orchestration of the negotiating process, including the language, timing and size of offers and proposals. This, in turn, signals to the other negotiator that you are unable or unwilling to make as many concessions as he or she thought possible, thus affecting his or her expectations about what kind of deal can be achieved.

Mediation: A process of conflict resolution in which the disputants attempt to negotiate a resolution to the dispute with the assistance of a neutral and impartial third party, the mediator.

Mixed Motive Exchange: The tension within each negotiator between competition on the one hand and cooperation on the other, as well as the same tension between negotiators concerning competition and cooperation. Strategic negotiating requires the negotiator to manage the mixed motive exchange—the tension between being cooperative and being competitive—in order to achieve his or her objectives in the negotiation.

MLATNA: "Most Likely Alternative to Negotiated Agreement." This is the most probable outcome if the negotiator does not reach agreement in the negotiation.

Typically, the MLATNA is what will likely happen if the negotiator walks away from the negotiation and tries to negotiate with someone else, or what will likely happen in court.

Move: An offer or proposal that a negotiator makes during a negotiation.

Negotiation: A process in which two or more persons communicate with each other in an attempt to reach an agreement.

Offer/Proposal: The negotiator's request or recommendation about how to reach an agreement concerning a thing of value.

Position: A specific proposal, stated by a negotiator, as to how an agreement should be reached. Example: "I want to purchase the inventory for $300 per unit."

Process: The way in which the negotiators negotiate. This involves the communication process between the negotiators. The process of the negotiation is referred to as "How" the negotiators negotiate.

Puffing: Exaggerating the benefits of a thing or of reaching agreement on specified terms. The purpose of puffing is to encourage the other negotiator to believe that he or she is receiving a good deal.

Short Circuit the Dance: When a negotiator attempts to shorten a competitive negotiation by "cutting to the chase" and giving up all his concessions. Typically, this occurs when a negotiator does not like competitive negotiating or lacks the strategic patience to engage in it. Short-circuiting the dance enables the other negotiator to compete for a new pie—the difference between the new concession and the other negotiator's last concession.

Strategic Negotiating: A conscious, disciplined, goal-oriented approach to negotiating. Strategic negotiating requires that the negotiator be fully conscious of his or her strengths and weaknesses, and that the negotiator uses language and self-management to orchestrate the negotiating dance in a way that best achieves his or her objectives.

Substance: The tangible, concrete thing being negotiated. It can be money, services, property, or any other thing of value that may be exchanged. The substance of the negotiation is referred to as the "What" being negotiated by the negotiators.

Tactic: A behavior by a negotiator that is intended to cause the other negotiator to react in a specific way. Tactics can be negative (e.g., yelling, crying, insults) or positive (e.g., humor, flirting, persuasion). Their goal is to get the other negotiator to make concessions that are not reciprocated.

WATNA: "Worst Alternative to Negotiated Agreement." This is the worst-case scenario available to the negotiator if he or she does not reach agreement in the negotiation. Typically, a WATNA means the worst possible outcome if the negotiator negotiates with someone else or goes to court.

Zone of Agreement: The range of possible outcomes that would be acceptable to both negotiators. The zone of agreement can be great or small. The zone of agreement is otherwise known as "The Dance Floor," that is, the range of possible ending-points of the agreement depending upon how the negotiators conduct the negotiating process. The larger the zone of agreement, the more room the negotiators have to dance; that is, to exchange concessions in their negotiation. Competitive negotiators attempt to reach agreements that are as far toward their end of the zone of agreement as possible.

Bibliography

Fisher, Roger and William Ury. *Getting to Yes* (2nd edition). Penguin Books, 1991.

Ury, William. *Getting Past No*. Bantam Books, 1993.

Lax, David A. and James K. Sebenius. *The Manager as Negotiator: Bargaining for Cooperation and Competitive Gain*. The Free Press (Simon & Schuster), 1986.

Axelrod, Robert. *The Evolution of Cooperation*. Basic Books (Perseus Books), 1984.

Raiffa, Howard. *The Art and Science of Negotiation*. Harvard University Press, 1982.

Norton, Eleanor Holmes. "Bargaining and the Ethics of Process." 64 *New York University Law Review* 493, 1989.

Hall, Edward Twitchell and Mildred Reed. *Understanding Cultural Differences: Germans, French, and Americans.* Intercultural Press, 1990.

Jandt, Fred E. *Win-Win Negotiating.* Wiley Publishing, 1985.

Lewicki, Roy J. and Joseph A. Litterer. *Negotiation: Readings, Exercises and Cases.* McGraw-Hill, 1985.

Warschaw, Tessa Albert. *Winning by Negotiation.* McGraw-Hill, 1980.

Wiggins, Charles B. and L. Randolph Lowry. *Negotiation and Settlement Advocacy: A Book of Readings.* Thomson-West, 1997.

Lax, David A. and James K. Sebenius. "Three Ethical Issues in Negotiation." 2 *Negotiation Journal* 363, 1986.

About the Authors

Matthew P. Guasco

Mr. Guasco is an attorney who is a professional mediator and arbitrator of civil disputes, including those involving complex commercial, employment, major personal injury, probate, and real estate litigation. He is an adjunct professor at Pepperdine University School of Law, Straus Institute for Dispute Resolution, where he teaches negotiation and mediation. Mr. Guasco has mediated and arbitrated over 700 disputes. He has also taught negotiation and mediation skills to hundreds of law students, lawyers, judges, business professionals, and governmental officials throughout the United States, as well as in the People's Republic of China and Hong Kong. Mr. Guasco lives in Ventura, California, with his wife, Susan, and his two daughters, Emily and Anna.

Peter R. Robinson

Mr. Robinson is managing director of the Straus Institute for Dispute Resolution and associate professor at Pepperdine University School of Law. He has presented advanced negotiation and mediation skills courses in more than 39 states and foreign countries. He has served on the boards of the Christian Conciliation Service of Los Angeles, Ventura Center for Dispute Settlement, Dispute Resolution Services of the LACBA, Southern California Mediation Association, and California Dispute Resolution Council. He is a fellow of the International Academy of Mediators, a member of the American College of Civil Trial Mediators and was recognized as a Southern California Super Lawyer in the area of mediation in 2006.

Index